BECAUSE OF CALVARY

TO: SKIP AND DIANNE,

"HIS MERCIES ARE NEW EVERY MORNING".

CLAIM THEM!

Charles Ray

ISBN 978-17-00377-76-0

BECAUSE OF CALVARY

A Year of Daily Devotions
Charles C. Ray

DEDICATION

For Carolyn Ray...I dedicate this body of work.
She has been my best friend for 62 years and my wife for 55 years.

Proverbs 5: 15, 18-19
"Be faithful to your own wife and give your love to her alone...so
be happy with your wife and find your joy with the girl you married –
pretty and graceful as a deer. Let her charms keep you happy; let her
surround you with her love."

My knowledge of the love of God is best explained and experienced
in my relationship with Carolyn. First, I know that she loves me, at
least as much as I love her. Because of her love for me, I can do
almost anything and she will still love me. However, because she still
loves me, I do not want to do just anything. I want to do those things
that make her happy and enhance her love...thereby increasing our
mutual love. Not to experience this with your life-mate is to lessen the
foretaste of God's love for us as His children.

FOREWARD

In September 2017, I was diagnosed with Angio Immunoblastic T-cell Lymphoma cancer and underwent chemotherapy treatment until July 2018. For several months, I was on oxygen, wearing facemasks, and mostly limited to my home. During this time, I was unable to go to church – even giving up my Presbyterian pulpit – but I never felt closer to God in my life.

The week after Thanksgiving, I began writing this book of devotions, concluding it in April 2018. This work was completed with prayers, challenges, discipline, and a cramped hand, as the 365 devotions were all hand-written on legal pads. My writing became a form of therapy, filling many days of almost total isolation.

I have many people to thank. My family became my greatest encouragers; friends too many to name prayed for me; and churches included me on their prayer lists. But the entire project was led by God's Holy Spirit – and thus it is – *Because of Calvary.*

CCR

JANUARY 1
SCRIPTURE: HEBREWS 1:2–3 (TEV)

"In these last days God has spoken to us through his son. Jesus is the one through whom God created the universe, the one whom God has chosen to possess all things at the end. Jesus reflects the brightness of God's glory and is the exact likeness of God's own Being, sustaining the universe with this powerful word."

The world has received from God Almighty, the greatest gift of all time; the gift of Jesus Christ. This gift is the reason for renewed hope for the peoples of the world. In Jesus, God has presented for each of us the way to be put right with God. Perhaps hymn writer John S. Dwight states it best in his song, "O Holy Night." He wrote, "Long lay the world in sin and error pining, till he appeared and the soul felt its worth." This one single sentence written by Mr. Dwight is full and rich with spiritual significance and Holy truth. God changed the total course of humankind in these words: "Till he appeared and the soul felt its worth!" The birth of Jesus was God's solution to our sin and "Error pining," which had for centuries ruled humankind's separation from Almighty God. Jesus brought to us the knowledge that "the soul felt its worth!" May your soul feel that worth this day and forever.

JANUARY 2
SCRIPTURE: JOB 1:1 (TEV)

"There was a man named Job who worshipped God and was faithful to Him. He was a good man, careful not to do anything evil."

Living a righteous life is the desire and call from God for believers, for each of us. Living a righteous life had to be God's desire for his people since early in creation. The Lord referred to Job as blameless and upright, one who feared God and turned away from evil. It would appear that righteousness might mean blameless, upright, or, in the New Testament, Christ-like in actions, deeds, and words. However, at the time of Jesus, there was great controversy about living a righteous life. God's people in the Old Testament felt all of God's laws were too numerous to obey. In the New Testament, Jesus Christ taught his followers that "You shall love the Lord your God with all your heart, with all your soul, and with all your mind; and a second is like it, You shall love your neighbor as yourself. On these two commandments hang all the law and the prophets." Thank you, God, for Jesus Christ.

JANUARY 3
SCRIPTURE: PSALM 100:1-2 (TEV)

"My song is about loyalty and justice, and I sing it to you, O Lord."

Christians are sometimes bent by circumstances beyond their control, but they are seldom broken. John Steinbeck, in his book *Travels with Charlie*, tells of traveling across the United States in his camper with his dog Charlie. Almost all the people that he met were unhappy, he wrote. They were unhappy with their vocations, the places where they lived, and many were unhappy with their lives in general. But Jesus wants people to be happy. He wants that for us - today! He wants our joy to be complete. The Lord wants us to be a part of an afterglow, not a part of an aftermath. An aftermath has calamitous effects (like a hurricane), and an afterglow produces a kind of glowing effect to our soul and being (like the birth of a child). One summer afternoon when I arrived at my house, our two granddaughters were playing in the driveway. The seven-year-old had written on the pavement with several pieces of colored chalk, "Dance with Joy, Sing to God, Live Life Smiling." When asked where she had read that, she said "I just thought of it." What a great way to live your life.

JANUARY 4
SCRIPTURE: ROMANS 8:15–17 (NKJV)

"For you did not receive the Spirit of bondage again to fear, but you received the spirit of adoption by whom we cry out, 'ABBA, Father.' The spirit himself bears witness with our spirit that we are children of God, and if children, then heirs of God and joint heirs with Christ."

Perhaps we as believers do not understand the person of the Holy Spirit, who along with God (the Father) and Jesus (the Son) make up the Holy Trinity. We hear the three referenced to and prayed to, as the Father, the Son, and the Holy Spirit. Recognizing the Trinity gives religious significance when we truly express our humble gratitude, thanksgiving, adoration, awe, and praise to our Creator, God!

The Bible tells us the "Holy Spirit" in-dwells in us. If you believe the Bible, then the Holy Spirit resides in us. Not only that, I Corinthians 3:16 asks us this question, "Surely you know that you are God's temple and God's spirit lives in you?" Do you know?!

JANUARY 5
SCRIPTURE: ISAIAH 49:15BH–16A (NRSV)

"I will not forget you. See I have inscribed you on the palms of my hand."

Foremost is God Almighty, who is the creator of this world and everything in it, including you and me. It was God who said, "Let there be light and there was Light!" And in the above scripture, God states, "See I have inscribed you on the palm of my hand!" Ephesians 1:9-10 tells us that God has a plan. "At the right time, he will bring all of creation together, everything in Heaven and on Earth, with Christ Jesus as the Head." Are you in God's Plan?

JANUARY 6
SCRIPTURE: REVELATION 21:7 (NRSV)

"I will be their God and they will be my children."

In reading Revelations, I have a difficult time making sense of all of the symbolism. However, there is great hope expressed in this book. Revelation ends humanity as Genesis opened it in paradise. The one difference in Revelation—evil is gone forever. What a culmination that John gives us to enhance and enrich our personal hope for eternal life: "He will be our God and we will be his children!"

JANUARY 7
SCRIPTURE: JOHN 9: 1–3 AND JOHN 9:10 (NRSV)

"As Jesus walked along he saw a man blind from birth. His disciples asked Him, "Rabbi, who sinned this man or his parents, that he was born blind?" Jesus answered, "Neither this man nor his parents sinned; He was born blind so that God's works might be revealed in Him."

"But they (neighbors and those who knew that he was a beggar) began to ask, 'Is this not the man who used to sit and beg?' 'I am the man.' But they kept asking him, 'Then how were your eyes opened?' He answered, 'The man called Jesus made mud, spread it on my eyes, and said to me, 'Go to Siloma and wash.' Then I went and washed and received my sight."

John 9:35-38—"Jesus heard that they had driven him out, and when he found him, Jesus said, "Do you believe in the Son of Man? He answered, "And who is he, sir?" Jesus said to him, "You have seen him, and the one speaking with you is He." Later the man said, "Lord I believe." And the man worshipped Jesus. The man knows Jesus simply as a man, and then he speaks of Jesus as a prophet. He finally comes to believe in Jesus as "the son of God." Many today have still not recognized nor accepted Jesus Christ as the Son of God. Jeremiah 29:13-14 (NRSV) tells us, "when you search for me, you will find me. If you seek me with all your heart, I will let you find me." **What a promise!**

JANUARY 8
SCRIPTURE: PSALMS 32:5 (TEV)

"Then I confessed my sins to You; I did not conceal my wrong doings. I decided to confess them to You, and You forgave all my sins."

While taking Communion, I looked down into my shallow cup and meditated on God's cost for my sins. A sincere request for pardon filled my being. Suddenly, I was amazed and somewhat startled at the reflection of three small lights in my cup. I had taken Communion in this church for years, but had never seen the three lights. I was thrilled in a special way. Even though they were reflections, at that particular time and in that particular circumstance, they were symbolic of the Trinity in my mind and heart.

My arm bumped the pew and tiny ripples in the cup distorted the calm, plain view of the lights, even though I knew that they were still there. Such is life, when we allow distortions to cloud or shake our faith in God. He is still there! We have only to be still and come with repentant hearts for God to forgive and set our hearts free…to see, as it were, His light in the calmness of the ripple-free cup.

JANUARY 9
SCRIPTURE: ACTS 9:1, 4, 5 (TEV)

"Saul kept up his violent threats of murder against the followers of the Lord. Suddenly a light from the sky flashed around him. He fell to the ground and heard a voice saying to him, 'Saul!, Saul!, why do you persecute me?' 'Who are you, Lord?' he asked. "I am Jesus, whom you persecute!'"

The complete life-changing mindset from persecution to recruiting Christians presents to us one of the most compelling and drastic changes of a human being recorded in the Bible. We know that he approved the murder of Stephen by stoning; that he was ravaging the church by entering their places of worship, dragging off both men and women and committing them to prison. Apparently, he appeared almost out of control in his zeal to persecute, punish, and imprison the followers of the Way. Nothing seemed to stop his pursuit of Christians. But Saul's life-changing encounter with Jesus, beginning with the light from Heaven, became a reality; and scripture tells us that within a few days Saul (now known as Paul) went straight to the synagogues and began to preach that Jesus was the Son of God. Paul's encounter with Jesus changed Paul from prosecutor to preacher. He knew who Jesus was in his head, and after his encounter with Jesus, he knew Jesus in his heart!

JANUARY 10
SCRIPTURE: JEREMIAH 31:33–34 (NRSV)

"I will be their God, and they shall be my people…. For I will forgive their iniquity, and remember their sin no more."

Forgive and forget are acts of human behavior that may be the most difficult to actually perform. When actions are directed toward us that hurt, we most often recoil, strike back, or plot revenge. God's attitude or actions toward the Nation of Israel certainly could have been any or all of these behaviors. The people were almost always disobedient to God's desire for them. How could the people still react with such dishonor? How many times did God have to remind his people, "I am your God and you are my people!" Why did they not understand God's desire for a love relationship? Well, God is God and He does as he pleases, and we very seldom do those things that God desires of us. God still forgives and forgets! That is the model that He places before us in our behavior toward others.

JANUARY 11
SCRIPTURE: PSALMS 16:3 (TEV)

"How excellent are the Lord's faithful people! My greatest pleasure is to be with them."

On a mission trip to Mexico, it had been our privilege to worship with a local congregation during their celebration service. Of course, the entire service was communicated in Spanish. We did not speak Spanish and most of the locals could not speak English. However, our group was invited to sing with the congregation. It was a strange sound, hearing the same tune sung in the two languages at the same time. Our united voices drowned out the little pump organ's sound.

I wondered how big God's smile must have been looking down and hearing this "joyous noise." Here we were, a group of Mexicans and Americans who had worked side by side for a week building a small mission church on the outskirts of Merida. The hot sun had been relentless as we worked daily under its burning rays. There we were, hot and sweaty, building frames, pouring foundations and floors and walls and roofs. There were very few words spoken but an abundance of gesturing and drawing on the ground. In spite of these handicaps, a small block building took form with all workers showing devotion to the job and knowledge of the end product. By the end of the week, we worshipped with them. Little wonder that the psalmist exclaimed, "How excellent are the Lord's faithful people."

JANUARY 12
SCRIPTURE: PSALM 139:1–3 (NRSV)

"O Lord, you have searched me and known me. You know when I sit down and when I rise up; you discern my thoughts from far away. You search out my path and my lying down, and are acquainted with all my ways."

In this scripture, David surely comes to this conclusion,
That nothing can hide from God.

> Death does not hide us from God.
> Distance does not hide us from God.
> Darkness does not hide us from God.

I can imagine that a blind man, having heard the 139th chapter of Psalm, could feel that someone is watching him. We all live under the watchful eye of God. Whether we regard that as thrilling or threatening depends on our way of life. Remember, the use of "Search" carries the idea of searching as if looking for something. God was and is looking for what he could bless, could approve of, and what he could reward in the lives of the Israelites. That is also his purpose for watching over you and me this very day and for the rest of our lives.

JANUARY 13
SCRIPTURE: I CORINTHIANS 11:23-25 (NRSV)

"Jesus took a loaf of bread, and when He had given thanks, He broke it and said, 'This is my body broken for you. Do this in remembrance of me.' In the same manner He took the cup also, saying, 'This cup is the new covenant in my blood. Do this, as often as you drink, in remembrance of me.'"

Why remember? Think about this, we all like to be remembered. Think how you felt when someone whom you thought well of, upon a second meeting says to you, "I'm sorry, I don't remember you!" In remembering, we recall to mind that which we had retained in our memory. I recall a country song that requested, "Don't forget to remember me." This is essentially what Jesus said to His disciples as He shared the "Last Supper."

Jesus wanted them to remember Him, but perhaps more importantly, He wanted them to remember the significance of the act of Communion. The Lord's Supper is a visible representation of the good news of Christ's death and His resurrection. (Jesus ends this act with the words "until He comes.") No matter how many times you partake of Communion, Jesus always wants you to remember Him and the act.

JANUARY 14
SCRIPTURE: ROMANS 12:9–13 (NRSV)

"Let love be genuine; hate what is evil, hold fast to what is good; Love one another with mutual affection; outdo one another in showing honor. Do not lag in zeal, be ardent in spirit, serve the Lord. Rejoice in hope, be patient in suffering, persevere in prayer. Contribute to the needs of the Saints; extend hospitality to strangers."

In the book *Les Miserables* by Victor Hugo, the main character, Jean Valjean, has just been released from 19 years in prison for stealing a loaf of bread. In his wanderings in the cities he is unable to buy food or lodging, turned away in neighborhoods, barked at by dogs, and found repulsive by everyone who sees him. Jean Valjean happens upon the cottage of a priest. After a knock upon the door, he is invited to "come in" by the priest. Jean Valjean introduces himself (honestly) as a convict having served 19 years in prison. Having just been set free only four days before, he asks the priest, "Can I stay here?" The priest invites him to the silver-plated tables, gives him a warm meal, and offers him a bed with clean linens, all of which Valjean gladly accepts. During the night, Valjean plots to steal all the silver plates and tableware so he can sell them and continue to wander. But he is caught by officials with the silverware and plates and returned to the priest's residence to confess, after which he is supposed to be carried to jail for stealing. In the presence of the law the priest not only gives Valjean the silverware and plates, but also the matching candlesticks. Then the officials release Valjean after this remarkable statement by the priest. "I have for a long time wrongfully withheld this silver; it belonged to the poor. Who was this man, Valjean? A poor man evidently." Then the priest says, "My brother, you belong no longer to evil, but to good. It is your soul that I am buying for you…. I withdraw it from dark thoughts and from the spirit of evil, and I give it to God!" Is not the life of Jean Valjean a clear reflection of what God gives us when we accept Jesus Christ as our personal Savior?

JANUARY 15
SCRIPTURE: GENESIS 1:3 (TEV)

"Then God said, 'Let there be light;' and there was light."

If the world's circumstances ever cause you to wonder about who is in control, reread the first three verses of Genesis, Chapter 1, and focus on the third verse. We cannot even imagine the power of God, who by His own will created and released light…and there was light. That act has both physical and spiritual significance that bares our constant thanksgiving. Physically, we do not have to live and have our being on an Earth that "was a formless void and darkness covered the face of the deep." The physical limitations placed on us by total darkness are too huge for us to comprehend. Hardly any living thing thrives in darkness.

Spiritually, the light is Jesus Christ, who says, "I am the light of the world." We are admonished not to hide our light under a basket, meaning that we each have some God-given possibility for reflecting His light. Now, we can't be John Wesley, John Calvin, or Billy Graham. That does not, however, relieve us of casting our light out to those in spiritual darkness or sharing with our friends and neighbors. Just think, you and I have that light! That gives us hope and responsibility. If the lightning bug satisfies God's plan as does the sun, then we really don't need to be a spiritual superstar to let our light shine.

JANUARY 16
SCRIPTURE: JOSHUA 14:9 (NRSV)

"And Moses swore on that day, saying, 'Surely the land on which your foot has trodden shall be an inheritance for you and your children forever, because you have wholeheartedly followed the Lord my God."

Life has its way of providing challenges for each of us. In fact, almost daily we are given challenges that require our conscious efforts to approach and to conquer. Some are easily met; others take a tremendous amount of courage to successfully overcome. Still others subdue us and we have to take an alternate direction. I like *opportunity* as a word to define challenge. It suggests that the challenge is an option that we make for ourselves.

We need to consider the selection of spiritual challenges as requests for ourselves, as opposed to those that life just presents. I believe that God not only helps us to meet these challenges, he richly blesses our efforts.

JANUARY 17
SCRIPTURE: 2 CORINTHIANS 3–4 (TEV)

"Let us give thanks to the God and Father of our Lord Jesus Christ, the merciful Father, the God from whom all help comes! He helps us in all our troubles, using the same help we ourselves have received from God."

Several years ago, I served as a counselor at a shelter for abused women. As a pastor at a nearby church, I would also invite them to attend our church. One of the ladies accepted that invitation and attended for five weeks. At her last meeting with me, she gave me a letter to read the next Sunday to our congregation. This is a copy of Glenda's letter to our church:

"Good morning, this is Glenda. I'm going to be writing a few words from my unique heart. First time I came to this church, I thought it was going to be like so many churches that I have went through, meaning I didn't feel comfortable. Trying to make me feel like I had to play a role to fit-in as accepted. But I realize God didn't make a mistake when he made me. So when I came to this church, this preacher and his lovely wife made me feel comfortable. I felt comfortable to be me. And I started to meet other members of the church. They also made me feel the same. It made me have a good feeling inside. I found my temporary church again. I was excited to come to church on Sundays to be around good spirited people, but as my life goes, it's always a temporary place. I've always been on the go. I've liked, you, I've met a lot of good spirited people there and I've always kept them in my heart like I'm going to keep y'all. So as I leave here, I'll have to go through the dangers the world have, but I know that I've always gone through it without the weapons of the world by the power of believing in God. So as I leave, I thank you all for making me feel welcome. Glenda

P.S. Until God says I have to go home, I'll see you one day again and as you remember me, put a smile on your face."

Our church, for Glenda, was "a community capable of absorbing her grief," and they didn't even know it until after she left the shelter.

JANUARY 18
SCRIPTURE: JOB 14: 15–17
(PART OF JOB'S DIALOGUE)(TEV)

"Then you will call, and I will answer, and you will be pleased with me, your creature. Then you will watch every step I take, but you will not keep track of my sins. You will forgive them and put them away; you will wipe out all the wrongs I have done."

These three verses once again demonstrate God's love for us:

> He will call…
> I will answer…
> He will be pleased…
> He will watch my every move…
> He will not keep track of my sins…
> He will forgive…
> He will put my sins away…
> He will wipe all of my sins out…

This is an announcement of good news, initiated by the Lord, with all His expressed benefits for us. All it requires of us is to answer. Isn't that the way it always is with the Lord…so little on our part, so much on His part? Just think of it: acceptance, concern, attention, forgiveness, and renewal…all from the loving God who has the power to control the universe and yet the love to know and care about me! Great, gracious God, you do all this, for even me.

JANUARY 19
SCRIPTURE: LUKE 15–19 (NRSV)

"At last he came to His senses and said, 'All my Father's hired workers have more than they can eat, and here I am about to starve! I will get up and go to my Father and say, 'Father I have sinned against God and against you. I am no longer fit to be called your son; treat me as one of your hired workers.'"

There are three definitions of the adjective *prodigal*. They are: recklessly extravagant, characterized by wasteful expenditures, and yielding abundantly. The scripture above refers to the father's youngest son, who took his inheritance and went to the distant country, where he wasted his money in reckless living. Actually, one can travel to a distant country physically, which the son did, and one can travel to a distant country spiritually, which this son also did. Either of these actions can be done by separation of ourselves from the love of God.

After the son had squandered his inheritance, the scripture states, "He began to be in need" and " no one gave him anything." Finally, the son came to himself. He says to himself, "I will get up and go to my Father." The son even prepared himself for a plea to his father. "Father, I have sinned against God and against you!" When the son nears his father's home, notice the father's reactions:

> The father is watching for his son.
> The father saw the son coming.
> The father was filled with compassion.
> The father ran to his son.
> Then put his arms around his son.
> The father kissed him.

A joyful reunion, and the father never even responded to the son's rehearsed confession. Aren't these the actions that God takes toward us when after our sins, we confess, repent, and return to Him and His way?

JANUARY 20
SCRIPTURE: PSALM 34:4 (TEV)

"I prayed to the Lord, and he answered me; He freed me from my fears."

Does it matter if we pray? Do you ever wonder who hears our prayers? God in three persons, the Trinity, hears our prayer! In fact, in the three following scriptures, the Bible indicates to us that the Father, the Son, and the Holy Spirit all help us with one of the essential tenants of the Christian belief and life. The Lord said, "I was ready to answer my people's prayers...I was always ready to answer; Here I am; I will help you!" (Isaiah 65:1) (the Father)

1 John 2:1-2: "If anyone does sin, we have someone who pleads with the Father on our behalf Jesus Christ." (the Son)

Romans 8:26 tells us of the Holy Spirit's help with our prayers. "In the same way the spirit also comes to help us, weak as we are. For we do not know how we ought to pray; the spirit himself pleads with God for us in groans that words cannot express." (the Holy Spirit)

So, the Trinity is available to us, free of charge, to help us in our prayer life. And, if they were not enough, James 5:16 tells us, "Pray for one another, so that you will be healed, the prayer of a good person has a powerful effect." How great is our God to help us in this way!

JANUARY 21
SCRIPTURE: PHILEMON 6:17–18 (NRSV)

"So if you consider me your partner, welcome Onesimus as you would welcome me. If he has wronged you in anyway, or owes you anything, charge that to my account."

Paul is writing to a Christian friend, Philemon, requesting that he allow a runaway slave, Onesimus, to return to Philemon. However, Paul's request has a second radical request of Philemon. The request from Paul to Philemon: "So that you might have him back forever, no longer as a slave, but more than a slave, a beloved brother!" In view of the culture of the society of that time, the assignment of people to classes was practiced. No one was able to move beyond their class. It was a lifelong position assigned to a person by reason of birth. But Paul, as a believer, parted from this mindset of his culture and agreed with Jesus' message. All face and class barriers were to change for believers. Paul had declared in Colossians 3:11, "Here there is no Greek or Jew, circumcised or un-circumcised, barbarian, slave or free, but Christ is all and in all." Please note in the above scriptures that Paul offers to repay any debt owed by the slave. In fact, Paul states, "charge it to my account." Isn't that what Jesus does for us? He allows us to charge our sins to His account when we accept Him as our personal Savior.

JANUARY 22
SCRIPTURE: MATTHEW 6:34 (MESSAGE BIBLE)

"Give your entire attention to what God is doing right now, and don't get worked up about what may or what may not happen tomorrow. God will help you. Deal with whatever hard things come up when the time comes."

The National Anxiety Center in Maplewood, New Jersey, gives us the following list of most frequent cases for anxiety attacks: AIDS, drug abuse, nuclear waste, famine, federal deficit, global terrorism, threat of full-scale war, nuclear attack from North Korea, loss of job, and growing old, alone, and unwanted. How do we handle such anxiety in our daily lives? In one of Charles Swindoll's books, he defines anxiety as "The painful uneasiness of the mind that feeds on impending fears." In Luke 10:38-42, Jesus is talking with Mary and Martha (sisters) as Jesus visits their home. Martha welcomes Jesus into their home. Mary sat at the Master's feet to hear Jesus' teachings while Martha was pulled away by all she had to do in the kitchen. Anxiety apparently gripped Martha and she went back to interrupt Jesus' discussion and said to Jesus, "Master, don't you care that my sister has abandoned the kitchen to me? Tell her to lend me a hand." Jesus replied, "Martha, dear Martha, you're fussing far too much and getting yourself worked up over nothing. One thing only is essential, and Mary has chosen it… it's the main course, and won't be taken from her." The main course seemed to be that Mary seizes the moment to be with Jesus and Martha did not seize the moment because she was distracted by all her kitchen preparations.

JANUARY 23
SCRIPTURE: GENESIS 2:8 (NRSV)

"And the Lord God planted a garden in Eden, in the east; and there he put the man whom he had formed."

You would have to be completely numb not to experience the beauty of spring with its trees, bushes, and flowers that seem to fill most yards during this season. Three significant thoughts occur to me at that time of the year. First: God's gift to us of His magnificent nature is an act of His desire to fill us with His plan and demonstration of His creativity. Second: The spring season reminds me of God's control of the world as one season replaces another on His schedule. Third: Gardens are special places to till for planting or for a place to retreat and communicate with the Lord. Let's look at three gardens of importance and interest in the Bible. In Genesis, God displays for His garden in which he placed Adam and Eve. The description of the garden is a paradise with all that humankind could ever want. Adam was to guard it and cultivate it. However, the occupants of the garden were disobedient to God's plan and they were put out of the garden forever. The second garden was the Garden of Gethsemane, which sheltered the praying Savior on the night of His betrayal. Perhaps Jesus' most difficult prayer was lifted up to God in that place; "not my will, but your will be done." The third garden was the Garden of Tombs in which Jesus was placed after his crucifixion. We know that this garden became the scene of the resurrection. The stone was rolled away from the tomb on Easter morning. No wonder that we cherish gardens, even to this day.

JANUARY 24
SCRIPTURE: 1 JOHN 4:9–10 (NRSV)

"God's love was revealed among us in this way. God sent his only son into the world so that we might live through Him. In this is love, not that we loved God but that he loved us and sent His son to be the atoning sacrifice for our sins."

God is Love! How long have you known this dynamic declaration for the Bible? This was one of my favorite Bible verses from early youth when we had "Bible drills" in Sunday School classes. One verse was "Jesus wept." I didn't grasp the full significance of the verses, but if I was called on first, this verse was short and didn't tax my developing memory. Later in my preparation for the ministry, this outline was presented as a guide for sermon thought: a structure of biblical truth that would lead persons to becoming believers. How so? By presenting and answering these three simple questions: (1) What? (2) So what; and (3) Now what? In the scripture above, we easily see the three questions demonstrated and answered.

1. What? God is love.
2. So what? This has implications for our relationship with God!
3. Now what? The answer to this is a very personal one that provides eternal life for each of us.

JANUARY 25
SCRIPTURE: MATTHEW 18:23–27 (TEV)

"Therefore, the kingdom of heaven is like a king who wanted to settle account with his servants. As he began the settlement, a man who owed him ten thousand talents was brought to him. Since he was not able to pay, the master ordered that he and his wife and his children and all that he had be sold to repay the debt. The servant fell on his knees before him. 'Be patient with me,' he begged, 'and I will pay back everything.' The servant's master took pity on him, cancelled the debt and let him go."

In this parable, the king is compared to God. (The last verse of the parable states, "This is how my heavenly father will treat each of you.") This major question arises: Why did the servant's master take pity on him and cancel the debt and let him go? These factors should be considered: (1) The king knew that the servant could not repay his debt because the debt was too great. (2) The servant knew he could not repay the debt. (3) The servant's intentions were good—he wanted to repay the debt—but he just couldn't! (4) The king felt pity for the servant because the servant in effect repented. (5) Because the servant did repent, the king cancelled the debt and let him go. You see, the king knew the servant's heart…He believed the servant's plea…and forgiving the debt . God's grace also extends to us: When we go to God with our sin, with a repentant heart, and with a desire to change our ways of living, God forgives us.

JANUARY 26
SCRIPTURE: PHILIPPIANS 2:13 (NRSV)

"For it is God who is at work in you, enabling you both to will and to work for his good pleasure."

In Paul's letter to the Church at Philippi (2:15) he states that God wants us to "shine like stars in the world." In God's desire for us to worship him for all his goodness to us and living Christ-like lives, we find God's good pleasure. These actions on our part bring about joy in our lives. Many consider this letter as Paul's joy letter. The concept of joy or rejoicing appears sixteen times in the four chapters. He reaffirms this joy in Chapter 4:4: "Rejoice in the Lord always, I say again, rejoice." Paul points out that the spirit of love and devotion was what he appreciated most about the gift of support from the Church at Philippi. When we give to those in need, it not only benefits the receiver, it benefits the giver. (Interesting how God works out this principle.) It is not enough to hear and read the word of God; we must also put into action and practice. Paul asks us, if you have gotten anything at all out of following Christ; if His love has made a difference in your life; if being in a community of believers means anything to you; if you have a heart; if you ever cared...what are you doing about it?

JANUARY 27
SCRIPTURE: 1 TIMOTHY 4–7B (NRSV)

"Train yourself in godliness, for while physical training is of some value, godliness is valuable in every way, holding promise for both the present life and the life to come. The saying is sure and worthy of full acceptance."

In this scripture we learn that Paul is instructing young Timothy, who is a pastor and a missionary serving with Paul in making known the Gospel. This instruction should also be followed by all of us who profess to be Christian. We all need to learn to "teach with our lives" by examples of "the way" in our daily living. For others we can certainly be examples; in our speech, in our conduct, in our love, in our faith, and in our purity. Some may be young in our faith-walk; others of us have walked the walk for many years. Regardless, the examples are not beyond any of us. These actions require no money, no appointment, no special designation, no certification, no registration, no written tests. This responsibility is one of Christ-like living on your part. The end results will be pleasing God, helping others, and rewarding to self.

JANUARY 28
SCRIPTURE: MATTHEW 5:6 (NRSV)

"In the same way, let your light shine before others, so that they may see your good works and give glory to your Father in Heaven."

God is the higher light and we are the lower light. But as such, we are still capable of reflecting the light of the Lord to our families, our friends, and to others whom God brings our way in our life's journey. Philip P. Bliss, hymn author and composer, wrote an old Christian hymn entitled "Let the Lower Lights Be Burning." He had just heard D. L. Moody state in one of many sermons, this sentence jumped out to Him and thus the song: "Brethren," concluded Mr. Moody. "The Master will take care of the great lighthouse. Let us keep the lower lights burning." We then are the "lower lights" as our lights reflect the light of God, which has been described as the "Great Lighthouse" by Mr. Bliss. I once heard a speaker make this unusual statement at a conference: "God made us to leak goodness. God leaks goodness, grace, love, compassion on us to enable us to do likewise to others. If we compare ourselves as a sieve, that statement is made clearer to me. For you see a sieve is a utensil with many small holes to allow liquids to pass through. God wants his light to pass through our lives in a sieve-like fashion to others. Be sure to keep your lower light shining!

JANUARY 29
SCRIPTURE: 2 CHRONICLES 26:3–5 (TEV)

"Uzziah became King at the age of sixteen and he ruled in Jerusalem for fifty-two years. Following the example of his father he did what was pleasing to the Lord. As long as his religious adviser (Zachariah) was living, Uzziah served the Lord faithfully and God blessed him."

Because of God's blessings, Uzziah became a mighty warrior, commanding over three hundred thousand soldiers. He tore down walls and captured several cities. He built protective towers for his own city. He became so powerful that his fame spread rapidly to surrounding nations. But as Uzziah became stronger, he grew arrogant and full of selfish pride. He even defied the Lord by going into the temple to burn incense on the altar, which was forbidden except as duties of the priest. The story indicates that Uzziah became angry and immediately a dreaded skin disease broke out on his forehead. Then for the rest of his life King Uzziah was ritually unclean. When he died, he was buried outside the royal burial grounds. This story perfectly reflects that pride and apostasy (which is a stray from religious commitments) will follow. Proverbs 16-18 reminds us that "Pride leads to destruction and arrogance to downfall." And pride is considered to be the most severe of the seven deadly sins of life. Do not allow pride and arrogance to become the guiding light in your life.

JANUARY 30
SCRIPTURE: ACTS 2:36–37 (NRSV)

"Therefore let the entire house of Israel know with certainty that God has made him both Lord and Messiah, this Jesus whom you crucified. Now when they heard this, they were cut to the heart and said to Peter and to the other apostles, 'Brothers, what should we do?'"

After the coming of the Holy Spirit, Peter's address to the people who had witnessed the response of the believers were amazed. These people were sorry that the Messiah had been put to death by their own countrymen. Their acts must have created a deep sense of guilt; they must have thought of the wrath of God for this act; what they had done could not be undone; their guilt remained! Sin always oppresses the soul! In this state of trouble, they were amazed at God's offer of eternal life if they follow Peter's answer to their question. Peter's response is still pertinent for us today. "Repent, and be baptized, every one of you in the name of Jesus Christ so that you will receive the gift of the Holy Spirit. God's grace is available to all who put their trust and faith in Him, even us today!

JANUARY 31
SCRIPTURE: JOHN 9:1–3 (TEV)

"As he walked along, he saw a man blind from birth. His disciples asked him, 'Rabbi, who sinned, this man or his parents, that he was born blind?' Jesus answered, 'Neither this man nor his parents sinned; he was born blind so that God's works might be revealed in him.'"

We are much like the disciples in that we sometimes form our impressions of others and/or their condition. Impressions come in all forms based on our experiences, imaginations, attitudes, wishful thinking, false assumptions, mean nature, and on and on. They can prove to be false or valid. Impressions can lead to a person becoming judgmental, which is a sinful action that often leads to being critical of others. My first impression has so often been proven wrong and I have been guilty of labeling persons. Once you label a person it is often hard to move beyond that first impression. When you are forming your first impression, look at the person or situation before you place a label on them.

FEBRUARY 1
SCRIPTURE: ROMANS 8:31 (NRSV)

"What then are we to say about these things? If God is for us, who then is against us?"

We as Christians know that all good things come from God. He is Father of all believers. God floods our very being with these actions. God:

Foreknew the Believer

Predestined the Believer

Elected the believer

Called the believer

Conforms the believer
to the of Christ image

Redeems the believer

Justifies the believer

Indwells the believer

Seals the believer with
the Holy Spirit

Honors the believer

Blesses the Believer
Loves the Believer

Comforts the Believer
Bestows peace on the Believer

Supplies the needs of the Believer

Seeks the worship of the believer

Restores the believer

Someday he will gather all
believers in Christ

Someday he will reward
all believers

Someday he will glorify
all believers

(Composer of this list is
unknown by this author)

Who then is against us?

FEBRUARY 2
SCRIPTURE: PHILIPPIANS 1:6 (NRSV)

"I am sure that God who started a good work in you, will carry it on to completion until the day of Christ Jesus."

This scripture says to us that's the way God's love works! It opens to each participant the caring heart that God places in humankind at birth. It has always been true and always will be true. We often lose sight of God's free gift of grace extended to us. Our very nation seems to be headed toward self- destruction. Too long moral and spiritual principles have been sacrificed on the altars of pleasure and materialism. America stands at a crossroad and we need divine guidance, for our survival is at stake. Among other things, we as individuals and corporately need to: review our blessings, remember our heritage, and renew our faith. God still loves us!

FEBRUARY 3
SCRIPTURE: JEREMIAH 29:11-13 (TEV)

"I alone knows the plans I have for you, plans to bring you prosperity and not disaster, plans to bring about the future you hope for. Then you will call to me. You will come and pray to me, and I will answer you. You will seek me, and you will find me because you will seek me with all your heart."

Many people today are in exile from the Lord—not necessarily in the physical sense, as was Israel during Jeremiah's time, but in the spiritual sense.

There are many things in our society today that spiritually separate us from God. This separation usually results in sin; troubles with things, people, relationships, health, guilt, money, and the list is almost endless.

We can be in spiritual exile in our lives where we live every day. Jeremiah gives us a list of four solutions that will bring us back into a right relationship with God. The above verses contain that list. We can: Call upon God, Come to God, Pray to God, Seek God.

Then, God promises in Chapter 31:33b, "I will put my law within them and write it on their hearts. I will be their God and they will be my people."

FEBRUARY 4
SCRIPTURE: PSALM 149:1 AND
PSALM 150:6 (NRSV)

"Praise the Lord! Sing to the Lord a new song, his praise in the assembly of the faithful." "Let everything that breathes praise the Lord. Praise the Lord."

Praise is one of the elements of worship. It might be said that as praise increases, worship deepens. Stop and think! Our lives are filled with God's wonders, blessings, and love. Too many to enumerate. Such has been His gifts to his precious humankind since creation. His creation and the presence of you and me in that plan this very day is a gift too great for us to even begin to explain. I have to confess that quite often, members of a split church have told me that I saved the church during the fifteen months that I served them as pastor. Instantly, my pride wants to rise up and accept this statement as truth. But, just as quickly when my honesty overcomes my pride, I have to remind others that God only used me as his instrument to bring reconciliation and guidance to a happy continuation of that church. I am sure that you have had to call on the power of God to put down your own selfish pride. We must then praise God both individually and corporately for bringing us back into His way.

FEBRUARY 5
SCRIPTURE: MATTHEW 4:1–3 (NRSV)

"Then Jesus was led up by the spirit into the wilderness to be tempted by the Devil. He fasted forty days and forty nights and afterwards he was famished. The tempter came and said to Him, "If you are the son of God, command these stones to become loaves of bread."

Our scripture refers to the devil as the tempter. That name for the devil is indeed a descriptive one. For every temptation that we encounter in our lives is put before us by the devil. Have you ever noticed the word *devil* (less the *d*) becomes the word *evil*. The evil tempter is the initiator of temptations that come our way, and he excels in his presentations. These verses have great value and significance for us if we are to resist the flood of temptations that come our way during our lifetime.

"For it is written" Jesus responded to each of the devil's temptations. Verse 11 tells us that the devil gives up on the three temptations; apparently the tempter is unable to battle both Jesus and God's word. The scripture states, "Then the devil left him, and suddenly angels came and waited on Jesus." The lesson for us is this: food, miracles, and power are what the tempter offers to us also. We need to study God's word so that we know it and can use it defensively when temptations come our way. Dear friends, the tempter is still in business today!

FEBRUARY 6
SCRIPTURE: PSALM 139:23-24 (NRSV)

"Search me, O God, and know my heart; test me and know my thoughts. See if there is any wicked way in me and lead me in the way everlasting."

How can we not, then, believe that we are God's person, each one of us, after such convincing words from Holy scripture?

Max Lucado in his daily meditations entitled *Grace for the Moment* (Volume II) begins the book (January 1) with the thought "Packed for a Purpose." He uses this scripture from Exodus 35:35: "God has filled them with skill." Thus, he states that "you are born pre-packed." This morning's scripture validates our knowledge of the love of God for each of us. As prepared beings, God has given us the time to complete His mission for us.

When we plan to go on a trip, don't we do the same thing?
Pre-pack—cold weather — bring a coat!
Going to church—bring a suit!
Time with the grandchildren…bring a pair of sneakers!
By all means—bring your daily medicines and vitamins.

God has packed us on purpose, for a purpose! He desires for you to be free of guilt, free of fears, and free of death. These are the mountains he wants to move from our journey's path.

You are God's person! He has given you His son's life for your salvation. His grace for you is astounding.

FEBRUARY 7
SCRIPTURE: ACTS 16:14–15 & 40 (NRSV)

"A certain woman named Lydia, a worshiper of God was listening to Paul and Silas. The Lord opened her heart to listen eagerly what was said by Paul. When she and her household were baptized, she urged us, saying, 'If you have judged me to be faithful to the Lord, come and stay at my home. And she prevailed upon us.' (Paul and Silas were jailed for "disturbing our city," verse 40.) "After leaving the prison, they went to Lydia's home; and when they had seen and encouraged the brothers and sisters there, they departed."

The gift of hospitality is one of man's gifts that God gives to his people to complete the ministry of His church. The church and each of us individually need to practice this gift of hospitality for our own growth and the growth of the church. The next time there are visitors in your church, notice how members reach out to them. Is it done with open and welcoming arms? This act of hospitality may just be the welcome that begins that person's journey toward an experience with Jesus. Do not overlook or fail to recognize the power of a smile or friendly handshake. God will be blessed and so will you.

FEBRUARY 8
SCRIPTURE: ROMANS 7:18–19 (NRSV)

"For I know that nothing good dwells within me, that is in my flesh. I can will what is right, but I cannot do it. For I do not do the good I want, but the evil I do not want is what I do."

We know that we cannot go back in our lives and correct mistakes because life doesn't come with a rewind button. Many times, I have wanted to go back and change my actions or my words. Haven't you? I would be hard pressed to know which has caused me the most pain over the years—words misspoken or acts mis-conducted. Both create in our hearts and minds so much possibility for hurt administered to others including family and friends. In my case, my words or actions are hardly communicated or demonstrated before I know that I have wounded another. Paul then asks this true question: "What an unhappy man I am! Who will rescue me from this body of death? Thanks be to God who does this through our Lord Jesus Christ." Then he adds, "There is no condemnation now for those who live in union with Christ Jesus."

We know that God's grace and hope are bigger and deeper than disappointment. Let the light of Jesus Christ direct your path on your life's journey!

FEBRUARY 9
SCRIPTURE: LUKE 24:32 (TEV)

"They said to each other, 'Wasn't it like a fire burning in us when he talked to us on the road and explained the scriptures to us?'"

Look closer at these two men on their walk to Emmaus. It is the day of the resurrection and they are walking from Jerusalem to a small village several miles away. They are confused by His trial, His sentence, by the crucifixion that followed. He had been buried, yet His body had been missing from the tomb. Some women had been visited by angels. What's going on?

We don't have to have much imagination to sense their state of confusion, anger, and sadness. So they are doing just what we would be doing…they are talking. In fact, they are talking with such involvement that they almost did not see Jesus draw near and began walking with them.

Notice the change that occurs in their actions as they walk with Jesus and listen to Him during the walk. Jesus explained to them all that had been said about Him in the scriptures. How they must have listened! Can you imagine the joy and excitement?

I believe it is significant in this story that once Jesus starts His discussion, there is no recorded indication that the two men spoke. They listened. However, when they had reached the village and they did speak, their first words to Jesus were, "Stay with us." Stay with us…isn't that what we want? Jesus, stay with us. If we truly listen to Him, don't we also want to say, "Wasn't it like a fire burning in us when he talked to us?"

FEBRUARY 10
SCRIPTURE: PSALM 100:1–2 & 5 (NRSV)

"Make a joyful noise to the Lord, all the earth. Worship the Lord with gladness; come into His presence with singing. Enter His gates with thanksgiving and His courts with praise. Give thanks to Him, bless His Name."

We shall all become active participants in the worship of our Lord during a worship service. This can be done by:

- a. Fellowship with each other
- b. Join in singing of hymns
- c. Join in unison and responsive readings
- d. Join in the Lord's Prayer and Apostles' Creed.
- e. Extend well-wishes to others upon dismissal of service
- f. Daily prayer for members and others
- g. Visit when possible

Don't blame the pastor if you leave the service with empty feelings. Remember who should be the participants:

1. God
2. You
3. Others
4. Pastor

Acts 2:42 gives us the basic four elements of first century Christian worship. "They devoted themselves to the apostles' teaching, fellowship, breaking of bread, and to prayers."

We can safely say that our worship service today is built around that Christian model.

FEBRUARY 11
SCRIPTURE: HEBREWS 10:16–18 (NRSV)

"This is the covenant that I will make with them after those days, says the Lord: I will put my laws in their hearts and I will write them on their minds."

In a number of places in the Bible, God said, "I will be their God and they will be my people." We know also from the Bible that the Nation of Israel is claimed by God to be His people. But what about the Gentiles? They were all the other people, except for the Jews. So where does that leave us (you and me)? Are we then "God's people"?

As Jesus' beliefs, teaching, healing, and preaching began to be more wisely accepted by the Gentiles, they became the most fertile soil in which the Gospel of Jesus Christ took root!

As the Gospel spread, the Lord's commandment became a reality. He said, "I have made you a light for the Gentiles, so that all the world may be saved." That light was Jesus Christ. That light can and does shine in our lives too!

So we should never doubt that we (Gentiles) are God's children. We have been adopted as God's children and made right through faith in Jesus Christ.

FEBRUARY 12
SCRIPTURE: LUKE 11: 2–4 (NRSV)

"Jesus was praying in a certain place, and after he had finished, one of His disciples said to Him, 'Lord, teach us to pray.'"

This was an interesting request of Jesus. Could it be because they actually witnessed the results of Jesus' prayers? Could it be because they had seen blind people, epileptics, lepers, mentally deranged persons healed with just a word or prayer from the life of Jesus?

The disciples heard Jesus speak and pray as no man had ever spoken. They had been eyewitnesses to Jesus' miracles, His teaching, His healing, and His preaching. The disciples knew that Jesus "went to the Father by means of His frequent prayers."

Could they really be given such power? Would Jesus teach them to pray? He did, He will, and He still does!! In response, Jesus taught them this prayer that we now know as the Lord's Prayer!

> Our Father, who art in Heaven,
> Hallowed be thy name.
> Thy kingdom come.
> Thy will be done
> On earth as it is in Heaven.
> Give us this day, our daily bread,
> And forgive us our debts, as we forgive our debtors,
> And lead us not into temptation,
> But deliver us from evil.
> For thine is the kingdom, and the power, and the glory,
> For ever and ever.
> Amen.

FEBRUARY 13
SCRIPTURE: MATTHEW 16:13 (NRSV)

"Now when Jesus came into the District of Caesarea Phillippi, He asked His disciples, 'Who do people say that the son of God is?'"

On this road trip, the disciples comes to a crucial moment in the ministry of Jesus when he confronted His disciples with two critical, distinct questions. Question one: Who do people say that the son of man is (verse 13)? Jesus knew that the twelve men had traveled with Him for three years, had seen crowds of people being astonished by His teachings, His healings, and His preaching (feelings that they too had experienced).

Jesus now had the disciples alone on the road, away from the crowds and the control of the religious leaders of the day. He then asked the question and after several answers asked the question again. He said to them, "But who do you say that I am?"

See the difference? Jesus wants a specific answer (from you) rather than people in general. This is a monumental question of the disciples, of the whole world of Christianity, of the church, and of each of us. To answer Jesus' question, we must be willing to answer, "Jesus, you are the Messiah, the son of the living God."

FEBRUARY 14
SCRIPTURE: I TIMOTHY 4:7–8 (TEV)

"…Keep yourself in training for a Godly life. Physical exercise has some value, but spiritual exercise is valuable in every way, because it promises life both for the present and the future."

While I was walking at a rather fast pace around the neighborhood, a friend asked from his yard as I passed, "What are you in training for, some kind of race?" My out-of-breath reply was, "Just trying to keep in shape." As I continued, this question kept coming to mind: What am I training for? Then it occurred to me that I am in training for life! That awareness has taken on a more serious spiritualness for me.

Later in this fourth chapter Paul says, "Do not neglect the spiritual gift that is in you…" This gift must also be exercised. This spiritual fitness is not to be found in a rested, docile state, but rather should be characterized by action… give, watch, forgive, instruct, care, pray, learn, work, listen, rebuke, obey, strive, love. If we exercise and practice spiritual fitness, we will be God's people at our best. The National Interfaith Coalition on Aging defines spiritual fitness as "the affirmation of life in a relationship with God, self, community, and environment that celebrates and nurtures wholeness."

Keep on exercising…one…two…three!

FEBRUARY 15
SCRIPTURE: MATTHEW 5:1–2 (NRSV)

"When Jesus saw the crowds, he went up the mountain; and after he sat down, His disciples came to Him. Then He began to speak and taught them." (using the Beatitudes)

The Beatitudes make up a list of commandments, Christian values, and noble ideas that differ greatly from the world's views. The best example of each teaching is found in Jesus himself. If our goal as Christian is to become more Christ-like, the Beatitudes will challenge the way we live each day. In examining these teachings, we find this group of Jesus/ blessings are in direct contradiction to how the world expects us to live. These commands require us to be willing to give when others take, to love when others hate, or to help when others abuse. Are these actions that reflect our words and deeds?

The Beatitudes are not multiple choices; i.e., pick what you like and leave the rest. They must be incorporated into our very being as a whole. They describe and guide us to what we should do to be like Christ's followers.

FEBRUARY 16
SCRIPTURE: MATTHEW 28:19-20 (NRSV)

"Go therefore and make disciples of all nations, baptizing them in the name of the Father and of the Son and of the Holy Spirit, and teaching them to obey everything that I commanded you. And remember, I am with you always to the end of the age." (NRSV)

Could it even be possible, even for us, to carry His message to the world? Yes, it was possible and it still is possible, and over 2,000 years later, the message is still being carried to the world. It will continue to be carried to the world with the "end of the age." But the difference now is that it is our time to carry the message. The ball is in our court.

You see, if we have accepted Jesus Christ as our personal savior, we have been empowered by the Holy Spirit. You and I have the power and responsibility to witness for the Lord through the Holy Spirit.

We need only to:

1. Pray
2. Open our hearts and minds to the Spirit's leading
3. Act upon His leading
4. Expect that the opportunity will be forthcoming
4. Then, do what is necessary in our own time, and our own way

Remember, He gives us the Holy Spirit to be His advocate—to help guide us each day.

FEBRUARY 17
SCRIPTURE: JOHN 1:16–18 (NRSV)

"From God's fullness, we have all received grace, upon grace. The law indeed was given through Moses; grace and truth came through Jesus Christ. No one has ever seen God. It is God the only Son, who is close to the Father's Heart, who has made him known."

The power of God's grace is then seen in our acts of repentance and conversion. One of the books of confession of the Presbyterian Church (P.C. U.S.A.) tells us that true repentance is conversion to God through faith in Jesus Christ and as such is "a sincere turning to God and all good, and earnest turning away from the devil and all evil." Repentance is a gift from God! It comes to us through His power.

On July 20, 1969, Neil Armstrong was the first man to set foot on the moon and his first words were, "One small step for man—one giant leap for mankind." But the most marvelous step for humanity was when Jesus came to earth. Praise God!

FEBRUARY 18
SCRIPTURE: MARK 5:1–20 (NRSV)

On Sunday, January 22, 2012, I preached my sermon from the encounter of Jesus with the demon-possessed man with the unclean spirit (Mark 5:1-20). A number of those in attendance have requested copies of the poem I used to close the sermon. You will no doubt notice that the poem is about me.

To some degree, we all experience within our inner being conflicts that require a higher power for release. So was Legion, whose tormented mind and bruised body were beyond his own control or that of any man and he was left to suffer alone and friendless.

In our secret hearts we long for that higher power to set us free and give us peace of mind and strength of body that we may live in harmony with God, others, and self.

I AM LEGION

I am Legion when in my life, I judge others for the same sinful acts of disobedience that I commit and try to hide. TEACH ME OBEDIENCE IN MY SECRET HEART.

I am Legion when in my actions, I respond with disrespect and hostility toward my loved ones, friends, and others. TEACH ME PATIENCE IN MY SECRET HEART.

I am Legion when in my thoughts I dishonor the privacy and dignity of others. TEACH ME SELF-CONTROL IN MY SECRET HEART.

I am Legion when in my trials, I let doubt and insecurity rule my behavior. TEACH ME PEACE IN MY SECRET HEART.

I am Legion when in my prayers, I half-heartedly present petitions, forgetting God's amazing grace. TEACH ME FAITH IN MY SECRET HEART.

In Legion's life, Jesus banished the spirits and Legion was found sitting with the Lord. Within my secret heart, "arouse the love that comes from a pure heart, a clear conscience, and a genuine faith." Lord, allow me to open my secret heart to a fuller knowledge of your grace so that my life can more compassionately reflect your love. TEACH ME WISDOM IN MY SECRET HEART.

FEBRUARY 19
SCRIPTURE: JOHN 8:12 (TEV)

"Jesus spoke to the Pharisees again. 'I am the light of the world,' he said. 'Whoever follows me will have the light of life and will never walk in darkness."

Darkness and light are unable to occupy the same space at the same time. This is an interesting phenomenon of nature. As long as there is no light, darkness prevails. However, once light enters, darkness is reduced in direct proportion to the amount of light. The more light, the less darkness. But the reverse does not work. The darkness cannot extinguish the light. We may feel that our light is not important to anyone; that our light is flickering at best. We may feel we are too immature to help, are too old, have too little time to assist, or a hundred other excuses.

God wants our light to shine. We may not all be like Mother Theresa or Billy Graham. But, we all do have a light. God's creation includes huge sources and tiny sources of light. Each shines and each has a purpose. Consider this: the lightning bug satisfies God's plan, as does the sun.

FEBRUARY 20
SCRIPTURE: ROMANS 3:24 (TEV)

"But by the free gift of God's grace all are put right with him through Christ Jesus, who sets them free."

Grace is a difficult word to define. I have heard it described as God's Riches At Christ's Expense. In my own life, I like to think of God's grace as all those good things that God has given me because he just loves me. Things like life, parents, siblings, wife, children, friends, and a whole host of things that enhance my being in this journey of life…and most of all Jesus Christ, who has put me right with God. I certainly don't deserve these many blessings. There is no way I could have earned them. You see, God knows me, my secret heart, my frequent and daily sins, so why would he even claim knowledge of me, much less extend His loving grace to me?

God does this because he wants a love relationship with me (and with you!). His greatest desire is to love us. No wonder John Newton refers to grace as amazing in his song "Amazing Grace," written in 1779. Webster's definition of amazing is "to overwhelm with wonder and astonishment." Even those powerful words do not adequately reflect God's grace for you and for me. It is freely and lovingly bestowed on us because we are God's children and he loves us.

FEBRUARY 21
SCRIPTURE: PSALM 57:1 (NRSV)

"Be merciful to me, O God, be merciful to me, for in you, my soul takes refuge; in the shadow of your wings, I will take refuge, until the destroying storms pass by."

Refuge is defined in two ways: (1) a physical place of safety from danger, and (2) state of mind about being protected. Read I Samuel 19-21. You will see the story of David and Saul. First, Saul brings David into his trust; then he becomes extremely jealous of David; and finally Saul plans to kill David. David learns of Saul's plan and flees from Saul. At that point, David hides in a cave to prevent his own death. David did what many of us have done when in trouble, seek refuge in God Almighty!

Actually, David found both examples of refuge. The cave offered physical protection, and his prayer to God provided him with a spiritual state of protection. Our awesome God **still**, today, offers and provides us both types of security. Can you imagine that after some of our confessions of our most offensive sins, **God loves us still!** We can rejoice that nothing in life or in death can separate us from the love of God through Christ Jesus our Lord.

FEBRUARY 22
SCRIPTURE: LUKE 18:9–14 (NRSV)

"Two men went up to the temple to pray, one a Pharisee and the other a tax collector. The Pharisee prayed, 'God, I thank you that I am not like other people; thieves, rogues, adulterers, or even like this tax collector.' The tax collector prayed, 'God, be merciful to me, a sinner.' Jesus announced, 'All who exalt themselves will be humbled, but all who humble themselves will be exalted.'" The point of this parable is this: the Pharisee, the religious leader, was not honest with God or with himself. The tax collector knew who he was; he was honest to God and himself, and he confessed to God that he was a sinner."

Let us remember that we can sometimes be both a Pharisee and a tax collector in our own prayers. We are part honest and open; then we can be part dishonest and shadowed by darkness. Guess which part we want to project to family, friends, and others? The Pharisee was comparing himself to the tax collector. We shouldn't compare ourselves to other people; you compare yourself to Jesus and His way. Only when we acknowledge the emptiness of our poverty, hunger, thirst, and tears can we be filled with the gladness of God's grace. We need to choose which we will be in the presence of God and others—the Pharisee or the tax collector.

FEBRUARY 23
SCRIPTURE: I PETER 1:142 (TEV)

Scripture: I Peter 1:142 (TEV)

"You were chosen according to the purpose of God the Father and were made a Holy people by His spirit, to obey Jesus Christ and be purified by His blood."

Peter wrote these words to the Jewish people who were in exile after the fall, as a reminder to remain faithful to their call to a living hope.

For a long time I wondered about these three questions about myself: (1) "Who am I?" (2) "Why am I here?" and (3) "What is my purpose?" I believe that God wrote these questions on my heart so that he could say to me, "You are my child and I am your God." Because of this statement, I believe that God has a desire for us to be led to a guide for life of a living hope. There are five basic truths that tell us: who I am, why I am here, and what my purpose is.

1. I am chosen by God to be one of His people,
2. I am chosen according to His purpose,
3. I am thereby made a Holy person by God's spirit,
4. To obey Jesus,
5. To be purified by God.

One of the simplest ways for us to live and die in the blessedness of God's promise is to recognize and act upon God's ways. We do this by admitting to the greatness of our sins and wretchedness. How are we to be free from our sins, and what gratitude do we owe God for redemption?

FEBRUARY 24
SCRIPTURE: GENESIS 6:7–8 (NRSV)

"So the Lord said, 'I will blot out from the earth the human beings I have created—people together with animals and creeping things and birds of the air. For I am sorry that I have made them.' But Noah found favor in the sight of the Lord."

This verse 8 has always been a kind of mystery to me. We know so little about this man; the major knowledge though is that "Noah found favor in the sight of the Lord." To gain more insight as to reasons why God found favor with Noah, we need to read verses that follow our scripture, verses 9 through 22. We find these characteristics of Noah:

1. Noah was a righteous man (verse 9)
2. Noah was blameless in his generation (verse 9)
3. Noah walked with God (verse 10)
4. Noah followed the Lord's instructions (verse 14)
5. God established his covenant with Noah (verse 18)
6. Noah did all that God commanded (verse 22)

Number 3 above, "Noah walked with God," may give us a clue as to their relationship. God obviously explained in great detail how he wanted Noah to construct the ark. Also, verse 15 would indicate that Noah grasped God's notion. In finding favor with God, Noah also experienced the grace of God in that Noah and his family were the only human beings to survive the flood.

FEBRUARY 25
SCRIPTURE: MATTHEW 6:14–15 (NRSV)

"For if you forgive others their trespasses, your heavenly Father will also forgive you; but if you do not forgive others neither will your Father forgive your trespasses."

Forgiveness is one of the basic cornerstones of Christianity! A person who is forgiven for their sin is a person who can redirect their life, become a person of Christ-like virtues, and continue in fellowship with God. It too should be one of the values upon which we stand in every place, in every time. We need to know about it, believe in it, practice it, subscribe to it, submit to it, and promote it. Forgiveness!

Forgiveness was so important to Jesus that he placed great emphasis on it in the concept of the Lord's Prayer.

FEBRUARY 26
SCRIPTURE: PSALM 16:3 (TEV)

"How excellent are the Lord's people! My greatest pleasure is to be with them."

A faithful relationship with God enables you and me to have joyful relationships with each other. When fellowship with God is broken, what happens to the person? (1) he or she stops working in the light (Jesus' way); (2) rationalizes their sin away; (3) no longer abides with Christ. In other words, the requirements of our fellowship with God are broken. God has not changed, but we have! God is still a faithful God who wants us to put his gift of relationship with him and others.

FEBRUARY 27
SCRIPTURE: PSALM 32:5 (NRSV)

"Then, I acknowledged my sin to you, and I did not hide my iniquity; I said, 'I will confess my transgressions to the Lord,' and you forgave the guilt of my sin."

Remember in the creation account from Genesis that Adam and Eve, after eating the apple, hid from God because of their disobedience. Thus ended God's original plan for humankind. But the beauty of God's love for them is this: God came searching for them and calling for them. This action is the very nature of God that is always present in his love for us. God still comes today, searching and calling for us! He wants to extend to you and me the gift of forgiveness, which He has given since creation. God's forgiveness to us is a beatitude of forgiveness! This verse in Psalms includes these three elements: a confession, a song of thanksgiving, and an instruction of wisdom.

Notice that David is filled with joy at his gift of forgiveness from God. In fact, David is so happy that he begins both verses 1 and 2 with the exclamation, "Happy." His soul's experience of joy is fulfilled by God's forgiveness.

This Psalm presents for us today the steps that we must take to be made right with God:

- Recognize sin
- Confess sin
- Repent
- Accept Jesus as our Savior
- Change our lifestyle
- Live an abundant life

"Be glad in the Lord and rejoice, O righteous, and shout for joy, all you upright in heart." (Psalm 32:11).

FEBRUARY 28
SCRIPTURE: LUKE 2:49 (NRSV)

"Why did you seek me? Did you not know that I must be about my Father's business?"

Jesus was talking, in the above scripture, to his parents, who were looking for Him in Jerusalem after the Passover festival. He was only twelve years of age and already learning about His "Father's business" from the religious leaders and learned persons. His ministry, no doubt, indicated that his early training and learning were the guiding principles in His teaching, preaching, and healing in "doing His Father's business." The Father's business is planned for us today. He has built into each of us our own special gifts to accomplish His will. Doing the things of God's business should be priority one in our lives.

MARCH 1
SCRIPTURE: JOSHUA 23:3-4 (NRSV)

"You have seen all that the Lord your God has done to all these nations for your sake, for it is the Lord your God who has fought for you."

Notice how Joshua refers, in talking to the people, to God as "your God." He does this two times in this scripture. Joshua is trying to stress how God has been involved in their entrance into the land of Promise. God wants the people to inhabit this land because he had promised it to them.

The early prophets and writers of the Old Testament, in trying to place emphasis on God and His faithful people, directed their thoughts of God specifically as your God. Believers of today know our God through His Son, Jesus Christ. Call upon Christ as your guide to God's way.

MARCH 2
SCRIPTURE: JOHN 14:6 (NRSV)

"Jesus said to Thomas, 'I am the way, and the truth, and the life. No one comes to the Father except through me.'"

Why do some people still ask, "Why is Jesus so special?" Many good men have begun religious movements that have been accepted as "their" religion. Even the disciples at times did not completely understand Jesus. In John 14, Thomas makes this statement to Jesus: "Lord, we do not know where you are going; so how can we know the way to get there?" In this same scripture, Jesus says (verse 7), "If you know me, you will know my Father also." Then Philip says to Jesus, "Lord, show us the Father; that is all we need!" If you want to know God, you need to look very closely to Jesus. "He was the same as God!"

> Look at Jesus.
> Examine Jesus' character, His teachings.
> Experience His love, grace, and mercy.
> Respect His concern.
> Observe His invitation to follow Him.
> Believe His words, "I am with you always, until the end of the age."
> And finally remember His words, "The Father and I are one."

What better picture of God do we need?

MARCH 3
SCRIPTURE: I PETER 5-7 (NRSV)

"Cast all your anxiety on Him, because He cares for you."

No matter what translation of the Bible you read, God cares for you!

The <u>Phillips</u> translation of this verse says, "You can throw the whole weight of your anxieties upon Him, you are his personal concern."

Do you see that "You are His personal concern"? How much more intimate can God be toward you, than for you to be "His personal concern"? Many times we become so bogged down in our troubles, doubts, and miseries that we forget that God even knows about us. The Living Bible, about this same verse, says: "Let Him have all your worries and cares, for He is always thinking about you and watching everything that concerns you."

The <u>King James Version</u> says, "He careth for you!" If you take nothing from this devotion, remember these four words: "He careth for you." This is the distinctive truth of the Bible.

MARCH 4
SCRIPTURE: JEREMIAH 29:11–12 (NRSV)

"For surely I know the plans I have for, says the Lord, plans for your welfare and not for harm, to give you a future with hope. Then, when you call upon me and come and pray to me, I will hear you."

Have you ever been somewhere and were given a map of the place you want to visit or tour? The map may have a red arrow indicating "You are here." In the above scripture, God is reminding the Jews who have been in Babylon where they are. Not only that, God is telling His people to make the most of their circumstances. He reminds them what they need to do for a future of hope. On the surface, that may seem to be a strange command from God. He had allowed His people to be captured and scattered from their homeland because of their disobedience. But, remember, our God is a faithful God and He still loved them. He wanted them to continue their lives. So much so that He said to them, "I will fulfill to you my promise and bring you back to this place (Jerusalem)." He wants to reassure the people that they will have a "future with hope." God responds to a faithful people with His own faithfulness. Today, God wants to give you a future with hope.

MARCH 5
SCRIPTURE: ISAIAH 6:8 (NRSV)

"Then I heard the Lord say, 'Whom shall I send? Who will be our messenger?' I answered, 'Here am I! Send me!'"

In a very real sense, this sequence of action between Isaiah and the Lord is what happens when we have an experience with Jesus Christ and accept Him as our personal Savior. Remember, in your own life, God's saving grace being bestowed upon you.

Isn't this what happens to you?

> God—confronted you!
> You—confessed to God!
> God—comforted you!
> God—commissioned you!

We must well reflect on the troubles of our own and call on God to account. But our questions of God might become questions of ourselves. Pondering these challenges, we might hear God ask, "Whom shall I send?" Do we dare answer, "Here I am—send me?"

MARCH 6
SCRIPTURE: MATTHEW 9:11–13 (NRSV)

"'Why does your teacher eat with tax collectors and sinners?' But when He heard this, He said, 'Those who are well have no need of a physician, but those who are sick. Go and learn what this means, 'I desire mercy, not sacrifice!' For I have come to call not the righteous but sinners."

Jesus tells the Pharisees the reason for His comments in this scripture. "Go and learn what this means." Perhaps they should have been more knowledgeable about Jesus' comment since the statement was directly from the Old Testament. They should have been familiar as they were the religious leaders of that time. The book of Hosea has this statement: "For I desire steadfast love, not sacrifice, the knowledge of God, rather than burnt offering." Jesus was informing the Pharisees the practice of offering the burnt sacrifices was no longer an acceptable gift to God, as in the past. Jesus came to be available to all humankind, including you and me. God gives us plenty of opportunities, almost daily, to exercise Jesus' command "Go and learn." Ephesians 2:10, tells us, "God has made us what we are, and in union with Christ Jesus. He has created us for a life of good deeds, which He has already prepared for us to do." How great is that?

MARCH 7
SCRIPTURE: MATTHEW 8:23 (TEV)

"Then a man suffering from a dreaded skin disease came to Him, knelt down before Him, and said, 'Sir, if you want to, you can make me clean.' Jesus reached out and touched him. 'I do want to,' he answered. 'Be clean!' At once the man was healed of his disease."

Perhaps the process for initiating a request of Jesus is just so simple that we completely overlook it. Maybe, we cloud the request with statements fashioned in too many *these* and *thous*. Or could we, maybe, just have too little faith to even expect a response from Him? Look at this man in Matthew's gospel. His approach to Jesus is a great model for us to follow. These elements are present...

A need: The man had a dreaded skin disease.
A movement toward Jesus: The man went to Jesus.
An act of praise: The man knelt before Jesus.
A declaration of Jesus' power: If you want to.
A request: Make me clean.

That rather simple request obviously made a significant impact on the Master because, He answered, "I do want to." He touched the man; and He healed the man!

It is reassuring to know that Jesus does "want to." Sometimes we lose track of His simple desire and we negate the relationship of love that Jesus wants with us. Let Jesus reach out to you today and say, "I do want to." Like the man in this scripture, the results will be life-changing.

MARCH 8
SCRIPTURE: HEBREWS 4:16 (TEV)

"Let us be brave, then, and approach God's throne, where there is grace. There we will receive mercy and find grace to help us, just when we need it."

You see, dear friend, God's grace is truly abounding for us to experience daily. And our response should be to give God honor and praise daily. Martin Luther expresses grace in this manner: "A very great, strong, mighty, and active matter is the grace of God. God's grace hears, it leads, it drives, it draws, it changes, it works all in man, and lets itself be distinctly felt and experienced. It is hidden, but its works are evident. Words and works show where it dwells." In my own life, I know of God's grace as all the good things that He has given me because He just loves me. He gives me among other things love, parents, siblings, spouse, children, friends, church, and the saving knowledge of His son, Jesus. I certainly do not deserve these blessings. There is no way I could have earned them. You see, the Lord knows me, knows my secret heart, my frequent sins, so why did He even claim knowledge of me, much less extend His loving grace to me? His greatest desire is for us to love Him. No wonder John Newton refers to grace as amazing in his song, "Amazing Grace." One definition of grace is "to be overwhelmed with wonder and to be astonished." Even those powerful words do not adequately reflect God's grace. It is freely and lovingly bestowed on us because He loves us. We are God's children!

MARCH 9
SCRIPTURE: MICAH 6–8 (NRSV)

"He has told you, o man, what is good; what does the Lord require of you but to do justice, and to love kindness, and to walk humbly with your God?"

The answer to these questions raised by Micah in the Old Testament has not changed since the time of His answer. We should still demonstrate these actions. We are able through experiences, communications, and relationships to worship God and to care for those whom God brings our way in our lives. These three requirements should help to prepare us for life's journey by establishing our purposes. It is a basic need to have purpose. The first question of the "Westminster Shorter Catechism" is this: "What is the chief end of man?" The answer is this: "Man's chief end is to glorify God and to enjoy him forever." Everything that exists was created by Him. Everything that exists is sustained through Him. Everything is given to God, meaning that it is for His glory. Let us all glorify God in our daily activities!

MARCH 10
SCRIPTURE: I PETER 2:10 (TEV)

"At one time you were not God's people, but now you are His people; at one time you did not know God's mercy, but now you have received His mercy."

In one of the confessions of the Presbyterian Church (PC USA), two points are made about the church; they are preparation and action.

Preparation: The church gathers; to hear His word, to baptize, to join in the Lord's supper, to pray, to present the world in worship, to enjoy fellowship, to receive instruction, to be tested, renewed, and reformed, to speak and act in the world affairs. These points may seem formal and stiff and handed down to us from the past. So, let's look at the church in which we worship and consider if we want to share these blessings with others.

We can worship God anywhere. But the church is where we worship Him in community. Do we want to say with the psalmist (16:3), "How excellent are the Lord's faithful people! My greatest pleasure is to be with them." The community of believers find in the church these blessings:

> a place to belong
> a place of security
> a place to be nurtured
> a place of forgiveness
> a place to be loved
> a place to pray

(This list was found in a copy of *Daily Living*.)

May your church be about and involved in these things.

MARCH 11
SCRIPTURE: MATTHEW 4:18–19 (TEV)

"As Jesus walked along the shore of Lake Galilee, He saw two brothers who were fishermen, Simon and Andrew.... He went on and saw two other brothers, James and John."

Jesus called to both sets of brothers with the same message: "Come with me, and I will teach you to catch men." Jesus' purpose, apparently, was to establish His own ministry, to select others to assist Him, to train them for service, and for these men to become full-time followers. As we know, Jesus selected eight more men and they became what is known today as Jesus' disciples. We still receive calls from the Lord today; not verbal calls. His calls are heard by the heart and not the ear. Have you ever acted on a premonition? This could have been a call from the Lord. It seemed to have come from God and it penetrated your heart and soul. Sometimes it provides motivation to acts of goodness and service. Perhaps it seems to override what you were otherwise thinking or doing. We know that God can do anything. Maybe He is softening your heart or sharing your thoughts to do His will. Something just told me!

MARCH 12
SCRIPTURE: JEREMIAH 17:5-8 (TEV)

"The Lord says, 'I will condemn the person who turns away from me and puts His trust in man, in the strength of mortal man. He is like a bush in the desert.'"
"But I will bless the person who puts his trust in me. He is like a tree growing near a stream and sending out roots to the water."

Through his prophet Jeremiah, God speaks of two groups of people: (1) those who trust in man and (2) those who trust in God. Essentially, these are also our choices as we live out our lives. We can either walk by sight, trusting man, or walk by faith, trusting God. Walking, trusting in man can often involve unloving and hurtful people; even family and friends can and often fail us. Walking, trusting in God assures us of blessings to us. For our scripture clearly states, "Blessed are those who trust in the Lord!" He does not want us to be like dried-up shrubs in the middle of a wasteland, but rather like a tree planted along a stream. There by the water one can be nourished in, to grow in Him, to become strong and productive. God wants us to be in touch with Him through prayer, worship, and His word. He wants frequent communication with Him. In fact, He wants you to have a love relation with Him.

I fall asleep so fast at night that I often am not able to finish my prayers. But you know what, I wake up several times each night, most times with a prayer on my mind. God, I believe, wants to hear from me. God gives me the opportunity to lift my prayers and he blesses me in return. Believers are a blessed people!

MARCH 13
SCRIPTURE: JEREMIAH 18:1–4 (NRSV)

"The word that came to Jeremiah from the Lord, 'Come, go down to the potter's house, and there I will let you hear my words.' So I went down to the potter's house, and there He was working at his wheel. The vessel he was making of clay was spoiled in the potter's hand, and he reworked it into another vessel, as seemed good to Him."

The use of clay was common to most people in biblical times and could be found in most households. The clay was used by a potter to create eating utensils, plates, bowls, and many other objects.

Clay was used because it was easy to recognize and commonly found to be fashioned into useful products. The potter's efforts were used by God to illustrate to Jeremiah how God could take a flawed person and rework him or restore him. Notice the restoration of spoiled clay was made into another piece, "as seemed good to Him." God is the potter and we are the clay. Jeremiah may not have been aware of this action on the potter's part until God reveals the significance to Him. Verse 5 tells us, "Then the word of the Lord came to me." Verse 6 says, "Can I not do with you, O House of Israel, just as the potter has done, asks the Lord? Just like the clay in the potter's hand, so are you in my hand, O house of Israel." And now, today, we are likewise in God's hand when we confess and repent!

MARCH 14
SCRIPTURE: II CORINTHIANS 12:9 (TEV)

"My grace is all you need, for my power is greatest when you are weak."

The desires and needs of the human being haven't changed much since biblical times. In verses immediately before verse 9, Paul indicates that he had a physical problem that bothered him to the extent that he talked with the Lord about it. In fact, Paul says he discussed it three times with the Lord. On the surface, the Lord's answer may seem unattached, unconcerned, or without feeling. Easy for God to say "My grace is all you need" when Paul is hurting. But look at the last phrase that God proclaimed: "for my power is greatest when you are weak." I don't think He means weak in the sense of exhaustion of self. Most of the time when we are in physical pain, we tend not to think of our inner self except for self-pity. We need to learn how to turn the self-pity to surrender to God so that His grace can be for us, all we need. Surrender in this sense, then, is not an act of giving up on stipulated terms that are initiated by us for our own interests or at times when our tails are in a crack. Surrender by faith is experiencing the very grace that is an unconditional gift of God.

For the meaning of this verse to work in my life, I must surrender self, experience faith through His grace, and receive His power.

MARCH 15
SCRIPTURE: GALATIANS 5:21–22 (TEV)

"But the spirit produces love, joy, peace, patience, kindness, goodness, faithfulness, humility, and self-control. There is no law against such things as these."

Think for a few moments on the last word from the list of the fruits of the spirit, self-control. While all elements of this list help throttle our thoughts, words, and actions and are gifts of God, self-control is the filter of the human soul. Self-control is the restrainer of one's thoughts, words, and actions. The control or lack of control of these three elements are generally indicators of our Christian or non-Christian beliefs. The Bible tells us that the desires of our human nature are usually sinful. They consist of passions and evil intent, and we are faced with making the choice that we sometimes have no control over. Sin enters into our being and those who have no self-control will not inherit the kingdom of God.

MARCH 16
SCRIPTURE: I JOHN 4:7 (TEV)

"Dear friends, let us love one another, because love comes from God. Whoever loves is a child of God and knows God."

I once read that there are two types of people in the world, those who come into a room and say "Here I am!" and those who come in and say "And, there you are!" Haven't we all seen both types?

First Type	Second Type
Says in words or action, "Look at me, I need attention"	Tell me about yourself
OR	OR
I am so important	You are important
OR	OR
The world revolves around me	I'm here to help you

Wouldn't the world be such a better place if there were more of the number two types (above). The Bible reminds us of this truth: "Beloved, if God so loves us, we also ought to love one another." I'm sure you have seen or heard the JOY acronym; Jesus, Others, You! Remember this JOY formula in all your relationships.

MARCH 17
SCRIPTURE: PROVERBS 3:5–6 (TEV)

"Trust in the Lord with all your heart. Never rely on what you think you know. Remember, the Lord in everything you do, and he will show you the right way."

At times we may try to alter our trust when the Lord does not answer our prayers as soon as they are uttered. At times we may think that He is indifferent, or preoccupied with other things or unable to act. His delay (if that occurs) has as its purpose the development of our trust in Him and Him alone for our good and His glory." Sometimes His will goes against our logic and common sense. The reason for this is to focus on our faith and trust in Him…not on our friends, or our own ability…or our resources, or our knowledge, or our strength, or anything other than Him alone!

MARCH 18
SCRIPTURE: ROMANS 3:24 (TEV)

"By the free gift of God's grace, all are put right with Him through Jesus Christ, who sets them free!"

The story about Adam and Eve in the Garden of Eden tells us that before they disobeyed God, the garden was perfect. There was no evil because there was no sin. When Adam and Eve disobeyed God by eating the fruit God had forbidden them to eat, sin entered the world (Adam and Eve and us). That is why no one has to be taught to lie, to cheat, to steal, to lust, to be envious, or to sin in so many ways. To sin is part of our very being and has been often referred to as our "sin nature." (For Paul's explanation of our sin, refer to Romans 7:14-25, entitled "the conflict in man"). This conflict comes in to our being sometimes for short periods of time, sometimes for lengthy times, and sometimes for a lifetime. We must take conscious, deliberate action by acts of repenting, confessing, and seeking forgiveness. We as believers know that God is in the business of forgiving! Paul asks this very question about the cause of his inner conflict. "Wretched man that I am! Who will rescue me from this body of death? Thanks be to God through Jesus Christ our Lord!"

MARCH 19
SCRIPTURE: MARK 2:10-12 (NRSV)

"'But so that you may know that the Son of man has authority on earth to forgive sins,' He said to the paralytic—'I say to you, stand up, take your mat and go to your home.' And he stood up, and immediately took the mat and went out before all of them; so that they were all amazed and glorified God, saying, 'We have never seen anything like this!'"

While this account of Jesus' actions in this scripture pertains to a physically paralyzed man, we know that Jesus can and does deal with one's paralyzed spiritual conditions. Jesus deals with our failures, our guilts, and anything else that presents to us a stumbling block to reaching and receiving the Lord's full blessing, intended for all of us. The Bible reveals to us that countless people through the ages have answers for their quests and their needs. The way to consider Jesus is to observe the things He did and listen to the things He said. Just in the Gospel of Mark, we see Jesus in so much action:

He cast out demons—He called disciples to fellowship—He cured a leper—He calmed the fierce winds of the sea—He raised a little girl from the dead—He walked on water—He told disciples where to fish—He multiplied loaves of bread and fish to feed multitudes of people! Jesus chose to do these things because He loves people. He is still in business today! Praise God! Look in the above scripture and notice the response of the people who witnessed the paralyzed man's actions. The scripture states that the people were amazed and praised God! And so should we be amazed and glorify God for His blessings in our lives.

MARCH 20
SCRIPTURE: LUKE 13:22 (NSRV)

"Jesus went through one town and village after another, teaching as he made his way to Jerusalem."

Jesus' decision to go to Jerusalem was certainly not to vacation; He was on a slow trip for the celebration of Passover. In fact, in Luke's Gospel, Chapters 9-20, are 13 pages of Jesus' teachings and parables. Jesus' mission was to reveal God the Father to the people so they could experience that love. He brought difficult ideas to those people through His parables, teachings, and healings. By examining Jesus' actions, principles, and attitudes, we can better understand the nature of God. This journey provides us with a fantastic opportunity to experience the Son of God in one of His most glorious times. You should read this account as soon as possible.

MARCH 21
SCRIPTURE: 2 CORINTHIANS 5:17–18 (TEV)

"When anyone is joined to Christ, He is a new being; the old is gone, the new has come. All this is done by God, who through Christ changed us from enemies into His friends and gave us the task of making others His friends also."

You are joined to Christ when you accept Him as your personal Savior. God then enumerates His actions; God not only changes us, he gives us the responsibility of bringing others into His way. We are enabled to perform this act by the empowerment of the Holy Spirit. You don't have to invent the Holy Spirit; the Spirit is already indwelling in our very being when we are followers of Jesus. We demonstrate our position in our words, deeds, and actions. Let us be about following Jesus in our total lives.

MARCH 22
SCRIPTURE: JOEL 2:13 (TEV)

"Come back to the Lord your God, He is kind and full of mercy; He is patient and keeps His promise; He is always ready to forgive and not punish."

There is an indwelling, longing in the heart of every person to know the eternal Lord and to have fellowship with Him. Every person needs soul satisfaction! For the Christian, it means that special attention should be given to our relationship with God. There is something distinctive about us as humankind. St. Augustine states, "Thou hast made us for thyself, O God, and our hearts are restless until they rest in thee." Our very nature compels us to think, and in that process of thinking, we are drawn to Almighty God.

Paul says in I Timothy 1:13-14, "God was merciful to me because I did not yet have faith and so did not know what I was doing. And our Lord poured out His abundant grace on me and gave me the faith and love which are ours in union with Christ Jesus." What then should be our response to God's grace given to us, His children? It is a known spiritual truth that you cannot worship and praise God when you are in rebellion with Him. The Lord wants us to repent sincerely and return to Him. Joel states, "He is always ready to forgive and not punish."

MARCH 23
SCRIPTURE: HEBREWS 12:1–2 (NRSV)

"Therefore, since we are surrounded by so great a cloud of witnesses, let us also lay aside every weight and the sin that clings so closely, and let us run with perseverance the race that is set before us."

Likewise, we as believers are surrounded by a great cloud of witnesses: When we are members of a church and when the church functions as Jesus designed it, we experience a community of believers like no other association that humankind knows or enjoys. Here is a good definition of the church: "By the grace of God, the acceptance of Jesus Christ as our personal Savior, and the empowerment of the Holy Spirit, we truly are gifted with the opportunity to worship God." Two of the living church's most significant elements that we can experience are loving and forgiving!

We need to consciously commit and recommit our lives to the cloud of witnesses who regularly surround us in the church as we worship God! It is there that we will find a place:

> To be nurtured
> To be loved
> To express our faith and concerns
> To be forgiven
> To be of service to the community
> To be about God's business!

MARCH 24
SCRIPTURE: I CORINTHIANS 13:12 (NRSV)

"Now faith, hope and love abide these three: and the greatest of this is love."

Let's consider hope for now. One definition of hope is this: "It is a desire accompanied by expectation." Accordingly, hope has two major components; to desire and to expect. To desire is to long for, to crave, to wish for. To expect means to look for as likely to occur. We all desire things. If you substitute the word *wish* for *desire*, think of the many times we say "I wish I could" or "I wish I could do that." Just think how many times you have wished for something this very day!

Having biblical expectations for the Christian has a stronger possibility because it has a promised expectation! We hold fast to the hope we have received in Christ, because our God is faithful. Hebrews 10:23 tells us, "Let us hold fast the confession of our hope without wavering, for He who promised is faithful."

MARCH 25
SCRIPTURE: MATTHEW 5:16 (NRSV)

"Your light must shine before people, so that they will see the good things you do and praise your Father in Heaven."

If someone looks at you, will they see a shining light that reflects the love and goodness of the Lord? God wants you to display yourself as on a billboard, so that your words and/or actions can be "read" and in doing so, make others want to know about the Lord you love. Billboards like people come in many forms: large, small, bright, dull, well lit, dark. Billboards play a major role in the scheme of marketing and advertising. Their purpose is usually an effort to get you to purchase something, to direct you to a location, to create an interest in a product. The advertiser uses vivid colors, flashing lights, moving parts, and a host of other attention-gaining subjects. They decorate the sides of most highways that you travel, maybe even more than you care to see; almost as much variety as there is in human beings.

In a different way, we are walking billboards. We are advertising ourselves either knowingly or unknowingly. Some in deep philosophical terminology, others in simple stated words. Some seem to want to "showboat" their actions; others just act in calm, sedate fashion. Does your light reflect the love of God in your heart or has your light been dimmed or shut completely off by weariness, loneliness, financial failures, or ill-handled relationships? God placed the light in you to shine. Remember, the children's song: "This little light of mine, I'm gonna let it shine."

MARCH 26
SCRIPTURE: MATTHEW 11:29 (THE MESSAGE)

"Walk with me and work with me—watch how I do it. Learn the unforced rhythms of grace."

Grace is defined (spiritually) as the love and favor of God toward human beings. One of my former pastors told me, "Preachers can never preach enough of God's grace." When it's sin verses grace, grace wins hands down. Grace invites us into life. We are weak and helpless because we can do nothing on our own to save ourselves. Grace comes to us as a gift from God. It is not a requirement, like a test or obligation. It is not a command, like an authoritative edict. It is not a duty, like an action that must be completed. The Lord said to Paul at a time of need in Paul's life, "my grace is all you need, for my power is greatest when you are weak."

MARCH 27
SCRIPTURE: PSALM 86:11 (NRSV)

"Teach me your way, O Lord, that I may walk in your truth."

In our journey of life, we sometimes walk the straight and narrow; sometimes we veer to the left and then to the right. Then we have to make corrections to gain or regain balance. Because of our tendency to be guided by our own agenda (our own way), we often waver on our route. Have you noticed that most new overlays on highways have noisemakers on the edges of sides to alert the driver that the vehicle is veering off the road? The reality of veering and correcting is necessary for reaching your destination. Our lives are also directed by veering and correcting to stay in the way of righteous living. Sometimes our highest spiritual strivings are interrupted by our veering off the correct pathway.

2 Samuel 22:31 states that "God's way is perfect." However, God, knowing His precious humankind, does not demand or expect perfection from us. When we are believers, God allows us to veer off the straight and narrow at times. And praise the Lord, He is the key to the correction of our mistakes.

MARCH 28
SCRIPTURE: JAMES 1:14–16 (NRSV)

"But one is tempted by one's own desire, being lured and enticed by it; then when that desire has conceived, it gives birth to sin, and that sin, when it is fully grown, gives birth to death. Do not be deceived, my beloved."

In Neil White's memoir *In the Sanctuary of Outcasts*, the true story about his rise and fall, this introduction appears: The author wanted the best for those he loved—nice cars, beautiful homes, luxurious clothes. He loaned money to family and friends, gave generously to his church, and invested in his community. But his bank account couldn't keep up. Soon the author began moving money from one account to another to avoid bouncing checks. His world fell apart when the FBI discovered his scheme, and the judge sentenced him to serve eighteen months in a federal prison." Mr. White actually spent his time in the "leprosy colony" in Carville, Louisiana, due to federal changes in their prison system.

Among the lepers he associated with daily were: a leper with no fingers, a man who would howl like a dog, inmates fat enough to be in a carnival, and a legless woman who chanted like Dorothy in Oz.

In reviewing his plight, Mr. White wrote, "Though I publicly acknowledged some of the bad things I had done, I had never taken an objective look at the person I had become. Finally, 'in a sanctuary for outcasts,' I understood the truth. Surrounded by men and women who could not hide their disfigurement, I could see my own." After his rehabilitation, Mr. White became a changed man and has become a Christian community leader in a new city.

MARCH 29
SCRIPTURE: 2 CORINTHIANS 1:20 (NRSV)

"For in Jesus every one of God's promises is a 'yes.' For this reason, it is through Him that we say the 'Amen,' to the glory of God."

God still speaks to us through the Holy scriptures. "A believer's stability for this life and for their confidence for eternity, rest solely on the written promises of God's word found in the Holy Bible" (source of this statement unknown). Remember that our God still speaks to us today! Among some of God's promises to us are these:

Joshua 1:5, "I will never leave you nor forsake you."
Psalm 32:8, "I will instruct you and teach you in the way you should go; I will counsel you and watch over you."
Isaiah 46:4, "I will sustain you and I will rescue you."
Genesis 28:15, "I am with you and will watch over you wherever you go."
Isaiah 49:16, "I have engraved you on the palms of my hands."
Leviticus 26:12, "I will walk among you and be your God and you will be my people."

Perhaps one of the most reassuring of all the promises of scripture was made by Jesus when he said to His disciples at Galilee after His resurrection, "And remember, I am with you always, to the end of the age." Hallelujah!

SCRIPTURE: DEUTERONOMY 29:2-4 (KJV)

"And Moses called unto all Israel, and said unto them, 'You have seen all that the Lord did before your eyes in the land of Egypt unto Pharaoh, and unto all his servants, and unto all his land; the great temptations which thine eyes have seen, the signs, and those great miracles. Yet the Lord has not given you a heart to perceive, and eyes to see, and ears to hear, unto this day."

The people according to Moses did not understand or perceive how God was working in the life of Israel during their domination by Egypt. To better understand the idea from Moses, we need to consider the word *perception*. I will use this definition of the word. Perception is a mental impression of something made by the senses to comprehend what it is. This type of perception is brought about by some action of one's senses; i.e., taste, hearing, seeing, touch, and/or smell. There is a second type of perception that Moses describes: the "Perception of the heart" given as a gift to us by God. Several years ago a friend of mine asked me to travel with him from Mississippi to New York State. My first perception of New York City presented me with a serious dislike, even to the extent that I never wanted to go there. He assured me that we would never see New York City as our destination was upstate New York. I went and found the people, the environment much like my own state. My perception of New York State had been based on a faulty impression about New York City.

I had seen so much about New York City on television that I never wanted to go there. I thought the state must be the same. A very faulty perception. It reminded me of Job's discussion with the Lord when he finally understood God's role in his life (43:3-5). "I talked about things I did not understand, about marvels too great for me to know. I knew only what others had told me. But, now I have seen you with my eyes." Job had experienced a spiritual perception, a real perception of the heart. You see, the perception of God's love is activated in our being when we acknowledge and accept Jesus Christ as our Lord and Savior. Rejoice and be glad and thankful.

MARCH 31
SCRIPTURE: JOHN 3:3 (TEV)

"Jesus answered, 'I am telling you the truth; no one can see the kingdom of God unless he is born again.'"

The majority of us are not in positions that require life or death decisions, although many of us make critical choices regarding other matters on a daily basis. We make choices, some small, some large, some almost without thought, some with much calculation and forethought. Each decision offers choices and we must be able to adjust to the results of our decisions. The choice is ours. It is when we do not act to make the choice that our destiny is guided by chance.

Each of us does have at least one life or death decision to make regardless of our vocation. That decision concerns our eternal life and it is the most important decision that we will ever make. God had formulated the plan for our salvation and has put it into action through His Son. Jesus has made the sacrifice, paid the bill, and cancelled our debt. If we accept Jesus by faith, there is nothing else we can do to add to God's gift to us and not in an effort to somehow earn God's love. Through His grace, God offers salvation to each of us. We need only to choose Christ in faith. That, then, is our decision.

The Reverend Max Lucado in his book "And the Angels Were Silent" makes this statement: "We cannot choose the weather. We can't control the economy. We can't choose whether or not we are born with a big nose or blue eyes or a lot of hair. We can't even choose how people respond to us. But, we can choose where we spend eternity. The big choice, God leaves to us."

What have you done with your big choice?

APPRIL 1
SCRIPTURE: LUKE 19:3 (NRSV)

"Zacchaeus was trying to see who Jesus was, but on account of the crowd, he could not because he was short in stature. So he ran ahead and climbed a sycamore tree to see Him, because He was going to pass that way."

Zacchaeus is sometimes identified as "the little man" who climbed up a tree to see Jesus as He passed through Jericho. He was not a believer or follower of Jesus, and simply out of curiosity climbed the tree to see Jesus, of whom he had probably heard. However, as we know, this little man was called out by Jesus, and Jesus invited Himself to Zacchaesus' house for dinner. Jesus said to him, "For the Son of man came to seek out and to save the lost." Any person who looks to see the Lord is in for a surprise. He or she will find that Jesus is looking for them.

APRIL 2
SCRIPTURE: DEUTERONOMY 4:9 (NRSV)

"But take care and watch yourselves closely, so as neither to forget the things that your eyes have seen nor to let them slip from your mind all the days of your life; make them known to your children and your children's children."

One of God's greatest gifts given to us is our memory. It is the faculty or process of retaining or recalling past experiences. We all know that we cannot remember all of our experiences. But, from early biblical writings God Himself and/or His prophets had admonished his people to remember certain acts, teachings, occasions, festivals, etc.... History has not always had the written word, or the Bible, as we have today to record happenings and to preserve for future reference.

But, you would think the people of ancient Israel would never forget God's blessing to them. Not only had God fed them with manna during their forty-year wanderings, brought them through the Red Sea, and delivered them from Egypt, He then brought them back to the land that was filled with lavish resources. Everywhere they looked, the Israelites could have seen God at work. Yet, they turned to worship other gods and forgot the one God who had led them and cared for them. No wonder God had to constantly remind His people not only to remember Him in events of their lives; He also admonished them to teach those same events to their children. A Russian philosopher once said, "Men have forgotten God." Is America headed in that direction today?

APRIL 3
SCRIPTURE: JEREMIAH 29:13–14 (NRSV)

"The Lord says, 'when you search for me, you will find me; if you seek me with all your heart, I will let you find me.'"

Worshiping God is a mighty gift that He has given to His people. And you gather each Sunday and for special events during the year to do that very thing. Worship God individually and corporately through your gathering, your praying, your singing, your Bible reading, your hearing the Word, and your fellowship.... These actions on your part are meaningful to God and honor Him as your Lord God Almighty.

I want you to consider this question, "Where do you see God at work in your church? In your friends? In your mission? In you inviting others to worship with you? In visiting the sick and shut-ins? Let's remember this: "God does His work through the church, through His people."

Look at the two brief statements of two churches who seem to acknowledge their belief that God is working in their churches:

"People come to the steeples because they assume that wherever there is a steeple at the top, there is a sanctuary at the bottom. People come to the steeples to find beneath the spires a room where fears can be voiced, sins can be confessed, tears can fall, questions can rise, and grace can accept. People come to the steeples hoping against hope that there will be a real sanctuary beneath the steeples. People come to the steeples to rest up, heal up, and start out again, nourished by the rituals they keep, the people they see, the hymns they sing, and prayers they raise, and the sermon they hear." (Rev. Charles Poole)

"Within these hallowed walls, the passages of life have been acknowledged, prayers have been offered, countless promises of commitment and love have been heard, the pain of grief has been shared, and reconciliation for broken lives has been discovered. Hungry hearts have been fed, anger set aside, new hope discovered, and simple vows made. This is a Holy place, and you are accepted here." (from a church in upper New York)

APRIL 4
SCRIPTURE: MARK 9:7 (TEV)

"This is my own dear Son—listen to Him."

Listening is a most difficult art. Let the conversation stop and you can feel the silence, almost becoming unbearable. In the scene of the transfiguration, Peter and the others were so frightened that they did not know what to say. Peter's remarks were untimely and maybe even inappropriate because he felt he had to say something. Then the voice of God was heard from the cloud saying, "this is my own dear Son...listen to Him."

Listen to Him! Peter, Peter, you don't have to put up tents: you don't have to talk among yourselves; you don't have to boast; "how good it is that we are here." Peter, you don't have to do anything...just listen. But then, we are all so much like Peter. That's why God's instructions to him are so meaningful to us today.

Listening to Jesus is our salvation and guide to successful living during our journey in this life. Just listen!

APRIL 5
SCRIPTURE: EPHESIANS 4:23-24 (TEV)

"Your hearts and minds must be made completely new; and you must put on the new self, which is created in God's likeness and reveals itself in the true life that is upright and Holy."

This scripture is speaking of a spiritual restoration of one's life after conversion to Jesus Christ. This means to return from sin to a spiritual state of being. He gave to us Jesus to model that state of being and the Holy Spirit to empower us to do such. The Lord created us and desires that we be in a spiritual relationship with Him. But our nature is like Paul writes, "When I want to do good, I do not; and when I try not to do wrong, I do it anyway. Now, if I am doing what I don't want to, it is plain where the trouble is; sin still has me in its evil grasp." Restoration is therefore required for us to be put right with God. Conversion is necessary for each of us!

APRIL 6
SCRIPTURE: PSALM 51:5 (TEV)

"I have been evil from the time I was born; from the day of my birth I have been sinful."

During the service of worship for Ash Wednesday, ashes are imposed on the forehead of the faithful to signify repentance before God, as related to us in the Bible. These words from Mark 1:15 (TEV) are spoken at the time of the imposition of the ashes upon the head: "Turn away from sin and be faithful to the Gospel." Ash Wednesday is a day of repentance and marks the beginning of Lent. According to the Bible, ashes were used to express mourning and sorrow for sins and faults. Repentance includes full responsibility for our sins. David said, "For I acknowledge my transgressions, and my sin is always before me.

Later in this same chapter (Psalm 51) David asks of God, "Create a pure heart in me, O God, and put a new and loyal spirit in me." Remember, repentance requires total honesty with God. Can you be that honest?

APRIL 7
SCRIPTURE: MARK 7:21–22 (NRSV)

"And Jesus said, 'It is what comes out of a person that defiles for it is from within from the human heart, that evil intentions come; fornication, theft, murder, adultery, avarice, wickedness, deceit, licentiousness, envy, slander, pride, folly. All these evil things come from within, and they defile a person.'"

In this list, Jesus tells the disciples (and us) that our thoughts and actions come from our hearts. They then travel from our very being by means of our tongues and our behavior. The Book of James tells us in chapter 3 about our tongues and our behaviors. In that same chapter of James he tells us, "The wisdom from above is first of all pure; it is also peaceful, gentle, and friendly; it is full of compassion and produces a harvest of good deeds; it is free from our judging and hypocrisy." We need to be concerned about our thoughts and be very careful to throttle our tongues.

APRIL 8
SCRIPTURE: LAMENTATIONS 3:21–24 (NRSV)

"But this I call to mind, and therefore I have hope: the steadfast love of the Lord never ceases, His mercies never come to an end; they are new every morning; great is your faithfulness. The Lord is my portions, says my soul, therefore I will hope in Him."

Right in the middle of the Book of Lamentations, we read of Jeremiah's grief, but he remembers God and has hope and states, "Great is your faithfulness." This scripture and this phrase became the theme of Thomas O. Chisham's song "Great Is Thy Faithfulness." You remember the chorus of the song: "Great is Thy faithfulness, great is thy faithfulness! Morning by morning new mercies I see; all I have needed thy hand hath provided. Great is thy faithfulness, Lord, unto me."

This hymn was simply the result of Mr. Chisham's morning by morning realization of God's personal faithfulness. God honors our prayers of thanksgiving. If God gives us blessings morning by morning, then should not we, His people, give Him our thanks, every morning? Each of us today could list a whole host of blessings that we have received from our faithful God! Be about demonstrating them in our lives!

APRIL 9
SCRIPTURE: 11 CORINTHIANS 5:19 (NRSV)

"In Christ, God was reconciling the world to Himself."

It has been said that the Golden Gate Bridge in San Francisco has two qualities that are also found in the Christian religion, namely foundation and flexibility. The bridge's two towers are built embedded into rock foundations beneath the sea. Also, the bridge is built to sway some twenty feet at center of the suspension span. Foundation and flexibility are the cornerstone of Christian life, found in Jesus Christ. He gives us our foundation and His forgiveness gives us flexibility. In our Christian lives, when we have experienced Jesus as our Lord, He then becomes the very foundation upon which we find our spiritual flexibility that allows us to accept the Lord's gift of forgiveness.

Because Jesus has forgiven us, we are to forgive others. In forgiveness we are able to demonstrate by word and/or action a willingness to yield. We can be Christ-like in our flexible attitudes toward those who might have grieved us. What a blessing!

APRIL 10
SCRIPTURE: MARK 9:35 (TEV)

"Jesus sat down, called the Twelve Disciples, and said to them, 'Whoever wants to be first must place Himself last of all and be the servant of all.'"

Jesus had heard the disciples arguing along the road as they discussed "who was the greatest." The above scripture tells us Jesus' reply. He is telling them that He is one who serves. The concept of the leader being a servant is totally foreign to their mind-set because Jesus was not only their leader, He was the Messiah. For the disciples and the Jewish nation, the Messiah was to be more like a king or one who would come and physically, politically, and economically rescue the people. He would overcome their enemies and establish peace, justice, and God's will. The people longed for this type of leader. They had waited and suffered for that wonderful time! So, why did Jesus continue by words, deeds, and actions to demonstrate and verbalize this business of the Messiah being one who serves? Jesus still tells us through the gospels that we need to place ourselves last and be a servant to Him and others. It still is difficult to understand and put into practice.

APRIL 11
SCRIPTURE: MATTHEW 8:1–3 (TEV)

"When Jesus came down from the hill, large crowds followed Him. Then a man suffering from a dreaded skin disease came to Him, knelt down before him, and said, 'Sir, if you want to, you can make me clean.' Jesus reached out and touched him. 'I do want to,' he answered. 'Be clean!' At once the man was healed of his disease."

I have heard, "We are battered instruments; life's strings have been snapping; life's bow has been bent. Yet if we will only let the Lord take us and touch us, from this old battered, broken, shattered marred instrument, He will bring forth music fit for the angels." All it takes is the touch of the Master's hand!

Through His covenant, God made it possible for His touch to be made directly to our hearts and minds, an ever-present possibility for each of us. That touch has occurred in each of us in different manners. Basically, we are touched when we experience Jesus and accept Him as our personal Savior. When we are converted, the Holy Spirit indwells us and empowers us to live a more Christ-like life. The testimonies of millions of Christians today can validate this touch of the Master's hand!

APRIL 12
SCRIPTURE: PHILIPPIANS 2:1 (TEV)

"Your life in Christ makes you strong, and His love comforts you. You have fellowship with the Spirit, and you have kindness and compassion for one another."

Consider the subject of attitude, more specifically, the attitude of Jesus. Here's a simple definition of attitude that I like. Attitude is the manner, disposition, or feeling with regards to a person or thing. Sometimes the attitude is often used to describe the ill-mannered nature of a person. Much has been written about attitude. Self-help books and articles go into great detail about how to develop good attitudes. It is good to remember these points about attitudes: we all have attitudes, they are easily recognized, they can be changed, and we need to make them positive. Let me give you an example of a good attitude: Several years ago the Auburn University football team used a small blue pin to attach to one's clothing with the word "attitude" written on it to emphasize the importance of a winning attitude. The team went undefeated while on probation, with no chance of winning the SEC title or to play in any bowl game. But, they had a super winning team and many said it was due to their attitude. Resolve today to be about imitating the attitude of Jesus' teachings.

APRIL 13
SCRIPTURE: JUDGES 6:14–16 (NRSV)

"Then the Lord ordered Gideon, 'Go with all your great strength and rescue Israel from the Midianites. I myself am sending you.' Then Gideon replied, 'But Lord, how can I rescue Israel?' The Lord answered, 'You can do it because I will help.'"

Gideon was in a winepress threshing wheat when an angel of the Lord appeared and spoke. In the New Revised Standard Version of the Bible, Gideon is called "mighty warrior." Actually, Gideon was a farmer. Can't you just see Gideon strutting around thinking, "I'm a mighty warrior." But when action was required, he quickly changed his attitude to doubt. Just as you would expect Gideon to do.

Gideon wanted a sign from God as to how he could defeat the enemy. Even though he had been told by the Lord, he still wanted more proof. Decisions for us today would be so much easier if we had more proof of God's will. Lord, just show me a sign!

APRIL 14
SCRIPTURE: JOHN 20:30–31 (NRSV)

"Now Jesus did many other signs in the presence of His disciples, which are not written in this book. But these are written so that you may come to believe that Jesus is the Messiah, the Son of God, and that through believing you may have life in His name."

Have you ever wished you could actually see Jesus? Touch Him, and hear Him talk? Are there times when you want to just sit down, talk with Him, tell Him about your cares and woes, or get His advice? Wouldn't that help when we have serious doubts? But then, God's plan is wiser. He has not limited Himself to one physical body. He wants to be present with each of us at all times. Through the Holy Spirit, He is with us, even now! You can pray to Him and read His words, even now!

Jesus tells us we are blessed if we can, and do, believe without seeing. We have all the proof we need in the words of the Bible and in the testimonies of believers and the eyewitnesses in the Gospels. I once saw a bumper sticker that read, "Read the Bible, it will scare the hell out of you."

APRIL 15
SCRIPTURE: ISAIAH 53:5 (NRSV)

"But he (Jesus) was wounded for our transgressions, crushed for our iniquities; upon Him was the punishment that made us whole, and by His bruises we are healed."

What? No burnt sacrifices, no gifts, no religious laws to obey? Simply astounding! Who would believe that God Almighty would choose to save the world through a humble, suffering servant? The people wanted a glorious King, a military genius who would slay all enemies; a ruler who would save all the people of God's own Israel. Now that kind of servant would be one whom was worthy to be presented with pomp and circumstance! But such a person was not in God's plan.

The people did not want a suffering servant and they did not even want to hear of one. The idea or even thought of a suffering servant was contrary to human pride and worldly ways. To the belief of almost no one, the Messiah's strength was to be demonstrated by humility, suffering, and mercy. Come on, Isaiah, give us a break!

APRIL 16
SCRIPTURE: MATTHEW 5:16 (TEV)

"In the same way your light must shine before people, so that they will see the good things you do and praise your Father in Heaven."

At our church's vesper service one night right after a tornado had hit New Orleans (about a hundred miles from our hometown) a frightened, disoriented, lady entered our sanctuary just as I was beginning to pray. And she interrupted my prayer by telling us her frightening story. Her home had been flooded by the hurricane and she had evacuated from her home in New Orleans. Outside of New Orleans, she got in the wrong lane of traffic on the expressway and ended up in our city. She came to our church seeking help. She was alone, never having been to our city. Her only companions were seven cats and a large dog. She told us, "I don't know what to do!" Someone asked her to be seated and we prayed for the lady. She stood up after the prayer and said she had to go somewhere and tend to her cats and dog. Instantly, and without question or comment, Susan (one of our members) stood up and announced, "I'll help you, come with me." They left the church and went to Susan's home, where the lady, seven cats, and the dog stayed for two or three days. The whole group at church at that time was as amazed as I was at the action of Susan. What a demonstration of Jesus' words. "Whatever you did for one of the least of these, you did for me!" Praise God for Susan's Christ-like act of love.

APRIL 17
SCRIPTURE: LUKE 10:36–37 (NRSV)

"'Which of these three, do you think, was a neighbor to the man who fell into the hands of the robber?'" He said, 'The one who showed him mercy.' Jesus said to him, 'Go and do likewise.'"

Jesus is saying to us, today, that the person whom we meet, who is in trouble, who is down on their luck, who is in need should be cared for as if our neighbor. We often have the opportunity to assist with the needs of people whom God brings our way, to be a good neighbor. There is something just so powerful about helping another person who is suffering or experiencing living problems. We are blessed when we assist them. Jesus says in Matthew 25:34-10, "Come, you who are blessed by my Father, inherit the kingdom prepared for you from the foundation of the world." For I was hungry and you gave me something to eat; I was thirsty and you gave me something to drink; I was a stranger and you took me in; I was naked and you clothed me; I was sick and you took care of me; I was in prison and you visited me." Then care for your neighbor!

APRIL 18
SCRIPTURE: ROMANS 8:16–18 (TEV)

"I consider that what we suffer at this present time cannot be compared at all with the glory that is going to be revealed to us."

We wondered many times during his last three months of life if bringing him home to die was the right thing to do. This was before hospice was in our area and we had little support, only his desire to die in his own home. With that desire foremost in our minds, we committed ourselves to that end. She cared for him during the day and I gave him shots every three hours, night and day. We worried about our three small children, perhaps going into Granddaddy's room and finding him dead. But, we prayed often and held things together as best we could.

We knew that he was safe in the Lord's love, but we often were helpless as how to comfort his physical pain. One day we were almost overcome with sadness and we went into separate rooms to read our Bibles and pray. My wife found this 18th verse and shared it with me. We felt that God sent us this word for our comfort…but better still, when we read it to Granddaddy, he smiled and thanked us for sharing this word with him. Now, I suspect that these words offered little relief from the physical pain, but what sweet relief for the believers' spiritual hope. We believe that Granddaddy rested in that hope and the whole experience was easier from that day forward.

APRIL 19
SCRIPTURE: I CHRONICLES 16:27 (NRSV)

"Honor and majesty are before Him; strength and joy are in His place."

You may be familiar with Nicholas Herman, better known to the world as "Brother Lawrence." He was not trained as a teacher, but he taught by his way of living, by practicing what he termed as the presence of God. He spent most of his life in a monastery in France, where he daily scrubbed pots and pans in the kitchen of a community of men. He never pastored a church or started a mission, yet, he is one of the best known spiritual figures in history. Brother Lawrence developed a habit of talking with God throughout the day, no matter what he was doing. He called it practicing the presence of God. His secret was to always know that God is near and to constantly talk to him. Here are a few of his pointers for practicing God's presence:

> Never forgetting that God is with you.
> Developing the habit of speaking with Him through the day
> Saying short prayers for people around you when you see them
> Praising and thanking God during the day's activities
> Confessing immediately any unworthy thought or instances
> Realizing that we are separated from God, even when we are
> working and even when we have sinned

We can do these same things when we practice the presence of God.

APRIL 20
SCRIPTURE: JOHN 1:4–5 (TEV)

"The word (Jesus) was the source of life, and this life brought light to mankind. The light shines in the darkness, and the darkness has never put it out!"

As Christians, we believe that God has placed in our very being that light and that we are empowered by the Holy Spirit to let our own light shine when we have confessed, repented, and accepted Jesus Christ as our personal Savior. If you have made these three acts in your life, the light is there right now, waiting to reflect the love of God. Jesus himself stated, "Let your light shine before others." That means that we all can be light that reflects God's way. I once read about light, that the lightning bug satisfies God's plan as does the sun! That means that God's light can vary from the smallest flicker to the bright sunshine. Nevertheless, God's light is capable of shining through our actions. This little light of mine, I'm going to let it shine!

APRIL 21
SCRIPTURE: ACTS 2:40–43 (TEV)

"Peter made his appeal to the people and with many other words he urged them to believe in Jesus Christ. Many of them believed his message and were baptized. They spent their time in learning from the apostles, taking part in the fellowship, sharing in the bread, and praying."

There are many methods of sharing the Gospel; among them are preaching, singing, teaching, personal testimony, and reading the Bible. It is by sharing your personal testimony that I want to emphasize here. Sharing personal testimonies is perhaps the most difficult for us. Just the word *testimony* often freezes our vocal cords. But we sometimes forget that actions speak louder. Pray that God will free you up to both verbalize and act out your spiritual testimony in relating the love, mercy, and grace of the Lord. We need to learn to share the good news thoughtfully, thankfully, and persistently.

APRIL 22
SCRIPTURE: HEBREWS 10:5–7 (TEV)

"When Christ was about to come into the world, he said to God: 'You do not want sacrifices and offerings, but you have prepared a body for me. You are not pleased with animals burned whole on the altar or with sacrifices to take away sins.' Then I said, 'Here I am, to do you will, O God, just as it is written of me in the book of the law."

The letter to the Hebrews was written to a group of Christians who failed with increasing opposition, and were in danger of abandoning the Christian faith. The writer encourages them in their faith. He did this primarily by showing that Jesus Christ was (and is) the true and final revelation of God. By means of experiencing Jesus Christ, believers are able to go to God without sacrifices, without burnt offerings, without going through spiritual leader or priests. The writer is explaining in these verses how Christ's sacrifice (his death on the cross) was a once-and-for-all gift to us. The animals and various other sacrifices could not forgive their sins, and neither could the priests. What they needed most was forgiveness…the permanent, powerful, sin-destroying forgiveness that was and is now available to us through Jesus Christ.

APRIL 23
SCRIPTURE: EPHESIANS 4:5–6 (TEV)

"There is one body and one spirit, just as there is one hope to which God has called you. There is one Lord, one faith, one baptism; there is one God and Father of all mankind, who is Lord of all, works through all, and is all."

God has chosen us (you and me) to be Christ's representatives here on earth. We have the awesome privilege of being called Christ's very own. This includes being humble, gentle, patient, understanding, and peaceful. People are watching our lives. Can they see Christ in you? How well are we doing as Christ's representatives? There is one body, Christian unity, and it doesn't just happen. We need to complement each other with our gifts and talents. Unity cannot exist in a selfish, self-centered state. "The disease of me" does not function as the church of unity.

The behavior of one or several in a group can easily break down the unity of a group, even in the church. Let us be about continuously striving for Christian unity in our churches.

APRIL 24
SCRIPTURE: ROMANS 8:8-9 (TEV)

"God's message is near you, on your lips and in your heart. If you confess that Jesus is Lord and believe that God raised Him from death, you will be saved."

Remember that Jesus Christ gave His life so that we may be put right with God. He initiated the opportunity to celebrate, as He did with His disciples, the sacrament of Holy Communion (the Lord's supper). We return to celebrate as the body of Christ. As the words express that, we should do it in remembrance of Jesus. The observation of Communion is multi-faceted:

1. It commemorates the Lord's sacrifice
2. It celebrates our salvation
3. It allows us to contemplate our sins
4. It challenges us to re-evaluate our lifestyle

Through these acts of commemoration, celebration, contemplation, and challenge, the Lord's supper becomes an important and effective aspect of the Christian life. Consider these points when you celebrate Communion!

APRIL 25
SCRIPTURE: PSALM 16:3 (TEV)

"How excellent are the Lord's faithful people! My greatest pleasure is to be with them."

In several of David's Psalms, he uses the phrase "in the assembly of God's people." He is indicating where he makes his expressions of peace to God. He is about sharing his joy and praises with the people, God's people when they are together. Notice the next time you are in the assembly of Christian people how many blessings your heart receives with their expressions of praises to God. Your imagination would be limited by your choice of expression of God's love and your unique response to His grace. You never know how your actions, words, or deeds may affect others.

Paul must have known about the scripture above because he states in Romans (1:11-12), "I want very much to see you in order to share a spiritual blessing with you to make you strong. What I mean is, that both you and I will be helped at the same time, you by my faith and I by yours." May it be also with you when you gather in the assembly of God's people.

APRIL 26
SCRIPTURE: JOHN 17:6–8 (THE MESSAGE)

"Jesus speaking to the disciples, 'I have shown your glory on earth; I have finished the work you gave me to do. I gave them the message that you gave me, and they received it; they know that it is true that I came from you, and they believe that you sent me.'"

Let me share with you three simple but potent phrases that will be extremely helpful in guiding your spiritual life:

1. Be grounded in the Gospel
2. Be secure in your hope in Jesus
3. Increase your love for others

If, in your daily life, you are able to successfully integrate these propositions, you will be living lives that matter to God, to others, and to yourselves.

God's gift of His only son is clearly presented in the New Testament, which is sometimes referred to as "The Good News." God reveals to us that His son Jesus died on the cross and rose from the dead to make possible a new relationship with Him. He grounds you in the Gospel, secures our hope in Jesus Christ, and increases our love for others. Praise God!

APRIL 27
SCRIPTURE: JEREMIAH 31:33–34 (TEV)

"This is the covenant that I will make with the house of Israel after those days, says the Lord. I will put my law within them, and I will write it on their hearts: and I will be their God, and they shall be my people...for I will forgive their iniquity, and remember their sin no more."

The prophet Jeremiah warned God's people of the catastrophe that was to fall upon the nation because of their idolatry and sin. The people were deported from Jerusalem into almost intolerable physical conditions. In this state of disarray, the people tended to blame others for the consequences of their very own sins. But Jeremiah reminded the people of this unpopular, but very true reality: "Everyone shall die for his own sin!" Every individual must regard himself as accountable to God personally. He then brings forth God's new covenant between God and His people.

Those who have accepted Jesus Christ as their personal Savior are granted or adopted into the family of God. In the darkness of God's children, through Jeremiah, He gave his people a bright and wonderful promise in his words. "I will be their God and they shall be my people." Since we, of the present age that have experienced Jesus, can say as it is written in the Book of John, "for the light shines in the darkness, and the darkness has never put it out."

APRIL 28
SCRIPTURE: 2 CORINTHIANS 4:16 (TEV)

"Even though our physical being is gradually decaying, yet our spiritual being is renewed day after day."

Sometime ago I read in *These Days* a page entitled "Re-firement in later years." The writer refered to retirement time as Re-firement time. His premise was this: there are three great temptations of growing old according to the article. "To whine, to recline and to decline." But the alternative to these three is spiritual; shine with passion and commitment. As long as God's fire burns in our hearts, we can render service to others, in our churches or communities. God's call comes at any and all ages. Henry G. Davis ran for vice president when he was eighty-two years old. His epitaph read, "He lived as if he would die tomorrow. He worked as if he would live forever."

Psalm 91:4 states, "the righteous will bear fruit in old age and are always green and strong." One study on successful aging indicates three marks of success:

1. Avoid disease and disability
2. Maintain physical and mental functioning
3. Continual engagement with life

But more important is the life of our soul. We need to grow most of all in our soul; growing in the inner life. Discover the inner strength that comes from continually seeking God's will.

APRIL 29
SCRIPTURE: JOHN 6:66–69 (TEV)

"Many of Jesus' followers turned back and would not go with Him and so He asked the twelve disciples, and you—would you also like to leave? Simon Peter answered Him, "Lord, to whom would we go? You have the words that give eternal life. And now would we believe and know that you are the Holy One who has come from God."

Apparently the multitude of people who were on the scene of this meeting determined that Jesus would not become a political leader. Many of this group would walk with Jesus no longer. Peter's question to Jesus is a profound one that has meaning to each of us even today. Many people go to various sources as a spiritual haven. Too often they find themselves confused and in situations that confound their search, increase their anxiety, and hide the truth and the way. Then it is on the way to another source, an endless, futile search. Peter had the answer! The only correct answer to the question "To whom shall we go?" Let us go to Jesus, who is Christ, the Son of the Living God.

APRIL 30
SCRIPTURE: GALATIANS 5:17–18 (TEV)

"What our human nature wants is opposed to what the spirit wants, and what the spirit wants is opposed to what our human nature wants. These two are enemies, and this means that you cannot do what you want to do."

We often find ourselves caught in some of the major dilemmas of our lives. What do we do with self? This scripture warns us that self wants to satisfy desires of human nature. We are momentarily repulsed by their implications and we say to ourselves, "I wouldn't do those things!" But sometimes later we find ourselves embedded in one or the other, maybe without much forethought and maybe without considering the consequences of our words and/or our actions. Our explanation to self and others is rationalization. "It's just human nature!"

As Christians, we know that God wants more than that from us. He wants us heart, mind, and soul; obedient to Him, loved by Jesus, and empowered by the Holy Spirit! Albert Einstein once said, "The true value of a human being is determined by the measure and the senses in which he has attained liberation from self." In Luke 9-25 (TEV), Jesus asks, "What good would it do to get everything you want and lose you, the real you?" Who is driving your life?

MAY 1
SCRIPTURE: I KINGS 3:5 (NRSV)

"At Gideon the Lord appeared to Solomon in a dream by night; and God said, "Ask what I should give you?"

Notice that Solomon loved the Lord and that he also used his Father's good name and reputation. His Father, King David, charged his son savings, "Be strong, be courageous, and keep the charges of the Lord your God." In his ascent to the throne, Solomon realized that He could make a request of God to bless him as he had blessed his Father. Solomon then states his own request of the lord: "Give your servant therefore an understanding mind to govern your people, able to discern between good and evil; for who can govern this your great people." Verse 10 of this chapter states, "It pleased the Lord that Solomon had asked." And the Lord said, "I now do according to your word. Indeed I give you a wise and discerning mind no one like you has been before you and no one like you shall arise after you." Solomon's request simply requested wisdom. That wisdom was from God, not knowledge and learning from scholarly pursuit. This is a beautiful account of God's grace and provisions. God is faithful in answering our prayers.

MAY 2
SCRIPTURE: 2 CORINTHIANS 5:5 (THE MESSAGE)

"The spirit of God whets our appetite by giving us a taste of what is ahead. He puts a little of heaven in our hearts so that we'll never settle for less."

While this scripture does not pertain to mothers specifically, the phase "He puts a little of heaven in our heart" certainly applies to mothers. It has been said that "God could not be everywhere at the same time, so he made mothers." Praise God for this special person in His plan for humankind. Just living confirms that being a mother is certainly not easy for her. Maybe some have even experienced mothers who drifted from God's plan for that little taste of heaven and plagued their children even into adulthood. If that is your mother's story, continue to pray that a loving and faithful God will forgive those mothers and bring you peace. I read these beautiful words (source unknown): "There is no greater thrill in life, than to point to that wonderful woman and be able to say to all the world, 'That's my mother!'" If your mother is alive today, tell her how much you love her. If she is no longer alive, thank God for her life.

MAY 3
SCRIPTURE: JOHN 10:1 AND 10 (NRSV)

"Very truly, I tell you, anyone who does not enter the sheepfold by the gate, but climbs in by another way is a thief and a bandit. The thief comes only to steal and kill and destroy. I came that they may have life, and have it abundantly."

I heard one morning on my car radio someone ask, "What are you doing?" The answer from the announcer was, "I'm just doing life," then he went on to explain. He explained that life for him was: getting up every morning, eating breakfast, driving to work, working from 8 to 5, drive home, eating supper, watching TV, going to bed; I'm just doing life, most every day." I would suggest that he's in a rut. We know from the Bible that Jesus wants more than the physical aspects of "just doing life." He wants us to add a spiritual element to our lives. He wants for us the recognition, the acceptance, and remembrance of God's grace that gifted us with His son, Jesus Christ. Isaiah 46:3-4 tells us, "I created you and have cared for you since before you were born. I will be your God throughout your lifetime—until your hair is white with age. I made you and I will care for you. I will carry you along and save you." In our spiritual relationship with the Lord, we are not only cared for in this earthly life, but in our eternal life as well. You will be on a higher plane because of the Lord's overflowing forgiveness, his abundant love, and His far-reaching guidance. Our cups runneth over!

MAY 4
SCRIPTURE: PROVERBS 6:27–28
(HOLMAN'S STANDARD BIBLE)

"Can a man embrace fire and his clothes not burn? Can a man walk on burning coals without scorching his feet?"

This devotional is directed to the male population because I believe that men sometimes get too close to the fire! I read of two fellows standing by a campfire on a cold, wintery night. One got too close and his pants were smoking. When his friend alerted him, the smoking pants man replied, "I couldn't even feel the heat!" He didn't remember the old saying "Get too close to the fire and you will be burned." Men (sometimes women) are not always able to resist temptation!

The only way to avoid getting burned is to be alert. The kind of man or woman God wants is a person who will follow Him and learns to love according to God's direction. Two basic characteristics of a person who pleases God is one who has internalized the God-given gift of loving and forgiving and who attempts to live a Christ-like life. What a privilege, what an honor, what a responsibility God allows us to be involved in…and you see, it's all about being obedient to the ways of the Lord.

MAY 5
SCRIPTURE: HEBREWS 11:1–3 (TEV)

"To have faith is to be sure of the things we hope for, to be certain of things we cannot see. It was by their faith that people of ancient times won God's approval. It is by faith that we understand that the universe was created by God's word, so that what can be seen was made out of what cannot be seen."

Wilmington's Guide to the Bible defines faith as a "superior principle of Christianity." The Book of Hebrews has been called the "Divine Hall of Fame and the Westminster Abbey of the scriptures." Look at chapter 10, verse 39. This scripture contains two very significant spiritual realities.

> It speaks to those who spiritually shrink back and then what happens to them: they are lost!
> It speaks to those who spiritually have faith. Then what happens to them: they are saved!!

Jesus Christ is both the founder and the finisher of the Christian faith. Considered these facts: Confucius, Buddha, and Mohammed founded three worldwide religious movements, but death finished these three. For our added strength, let us in our own lives and actions and prayers say to God: My faith looks up to thee!

MAY 6
SCRIPTURE: MARK 5:1–5 (TEV)

"Jesus and His disciples got out of the boat, He was met by a man who came out of the burial caves. This man had an evil spirit in him and lived among the tombs. Nobody could keep him tied with chains anymore…every time he broke the chains and smashed the irons on his feet…Jesus asked him, 'What is your name?' The man answered, 'My name is Legion, there are so many of us!'"

(Note to reader: Read Chapter 5:1-20 for the whole story.)

This man has a unique experience with Jesus. Look at Legion before that experience. The scripture indicates these facts about him: He was undoubtedly known in this region; he ran naked in his surroundings; was known to have an unclean spirit; shouted when he talked; knew Jesus was the Son of the Most High God; kept under guard; and was driven by demons in his actions.

Then, after his encounter with Jesus, he had a complete change in his life. He was seen sitting at the feet of Jesus, clothed, and in his right mind. He wanted to go with Jesus, begged to be with Jesus, and wanted to share Jesus' mission. Was this the same man? An encounter with Jesus brings about beauty within, and the beauty brings about a complete change in one's life. Let your beauty be seen and give God thanks and praise.

MAY 7
SCRIPTURE: JOHN 1:15–16 (TEV)

"John the Baptist spoke about (Jesus). He cried out, 'This is the one I was thinking about when I said, "He comes after me, but He is greater than I am because He existed before I was born."' Out of the fullness of His grace, He has blessed us all, giving us one blessing after another…. But grace and truth come through Jesus Christ."

These few verses by John the Baptist give us a clear picture of his spiritual position that he felt toward Jesus. A position that marked his life and eventually brought about his death. These facts are also enumerated in the Bible about this man. He was the son of Mary's cousin Elizabeth and his father was Zechariah. John was a well-known spiritual leader. He had followers and disciples. Many thought that he might have been the long-expected Messiah. He baptized his followers. He knew his spiritual belief and did not use it for gain for himself. We know his position, which he explained to the Pharisees: "I baptize with water. Among you stands one whom you do not know, the one who is coming after me; I am not worthy to untie the thong of His sandal." You see, John is not the message; he is the messenger and he is saying in effect, "Less of me and more of Jesus." He wanted them to get off his agenda and get on Jesus' agenda. Isn't that what our agenda should be in our own lives? More of Jesus and less of us?

MAY 8
SCRIPTURE: JOHN 10:28 (NRSV)

"I give them eternal life, and they will never perish. No one will snatch them out of my hand."

A reporter made this comment on December 26, 2004, after the South Asian region's unbelievable earthquake, "No point on each village remained undisturbed." As we journey, there remains a great chance that our own lives may experience an earthquake. Spiritually speaking, the scripture gives validity to the phrase "they will never perish" because the Lord gives us eternal life, here on earth as well as in the afterlife. We are held in the blessed, reassuring hand of God Almighty! Praise God!

MAY 9
SCRIPTURE: I THESSALONIANS 5:10–11 (NRSV)

"Whether we are awake or asleep, we may live with Him. Therefore, encourage one another and build up each other, as indeed you are doing."

Food and water are essential to the vitality of our functioning as a living being. Almost as important is the feeling of encouragement from others. We all need encouragement if we are to be happy and effective in our lives. Individuals, as well as groups, need the emotional, psychological, and spiritual boost of encouragement that a good word or a pat on the back or a hug gives you. Some of us would rate high on a rating scale for encouragement, others not so high, and sadly a few would not even move the scale.

I read a recent poll that reported that our "nation is in a decline in our function as encouragers." It was suggesting that we have become Lone Rangers in our spirituality. Church attendance is down, biblical beliefs are abandoned, and more and more people are looking inward (online, self-help books, etc.) and out of doors for uplifts that were once found in church. Those of us who are believers know that regular contact with encouragers provides us with emotional and spiritual assistance on a regular basis. Needless to say, we need each other, to offer encouragement. Don't become a spiritual "Lone Ranger."

MAY 10
SCRIPTURE: 2 CORINTHIANS 5:18 (TEV)

"God through Christ changed us from enemies into His friends and gave us the task of making others His friends also."

A devotional in a past magazine makes these three functions of friendship: commitment, communication, commonality. But these specifics he states by commitment: Jesus said, "You are my friends when you do whatever I command." He states by communication: Jesus promises to us that He will tell us all that the Father has told Him. He states by commonality: He will be sharing His glory in our attitudes and actions.

What a blessing it is to have friends—not only ordinary casual friends, but those special people that would give you the shirt off their back, so to speak. A friend who cries with you and laughs with you in joy. Thank you, God, for the sweet gift of friendship!

MAY 11
SCRIPTURE: JOHN 1:3–5 (NRSV)

"What has come into being in Jesus was life, and the life was the light of all people. The light shines in the darkness, and the darkness did not overcome it."

We know through the Genesis account of God's creation of the universe that He created light by His mighty power, which resulted in His command, "Let there be light!" And there was light! God saw that the light was good. So God gave us the physical light that lights our way every day. Humankind has enhanced light in so many ways. God also, as the scripture indicates, presented to us a far more brilliant light, that being His only son, Jesus Christ. Wow! God's spiritual light offers to each of us a never-ending light that can be each person's by simply accepting Him as our Savior! God wants Jesus' light to shine in you and through you.

It can be done by these three acts on your part:

> First, recognize Jesus (the light of the world)
> Second, receive Jesus as your Savior
> Third, responding in love to His love, His grace, His mercy to reflect to others

Let His light shine in and through you! Throughout the Bible, you can see these three functions of humankind at work: recognize, receive, and respond! Through these three actions, you move from darkness to eternal light. Choice, not chance, determines our destiny. Therefore, we dim our own light sometimes. Shine bright!!!

MAY 12
SCRIPTURE: PSALM 33:20–22 (NRSV)

"Our soul waits for the Lord; He is our help and shield. Our heart is glad in Him, because we trust in His Holy name. Let your steadfast love, O Lord, be upon us, even as we hope in you."

I read that one of the Hebrew words, *hope*, is also translated to the word *wait*. This Psalm is important to us because it indicates that we actively are engaged in both hoping and waiting. We believe in both because we know that God is dependable; we can remain optimistic about the future. Each value of the passage of time is allotted to us. At times we wait and at times we want time to speed up. Waiting helps us to develop patience and remember; patience is one of the fruits of the spirit! Even so, we sometimes have a hard time waiting because we want to do things on our schedule, our timetable, rather than in accordance with the Lord's time. Most of the time we spend waiting we are also hoping. Remember how we wait and hope for something: "Everything that happens in this world" happens at the time God chooses. God sets the time and gives us hope for the happening. Be faithful, wait, then be thankful for God's response!

MAY 13
SCRIPTURE: JOHN 12:20-21 (NRSV)

"Now among those who went up to worship at the Festival were some Greeks. They came to Philip, who was from Bethsaida in Galilee, and said to him, 'Sir, we wish to see Jesus.'"

These Greeks may have been converts of Jesus but had probably never seen Him. They had heard enough from the crowds, perhaps from the disciples, and now they wanted to see Jesus to listen and learn from the real source. While in the crowd, they heard Jesus say, "Father, glorify your name." Then a voice came from Heaven: "I have glorified it and I will glorify it again." The crowd that was present said it was an angel who had spoken; others said it was thunder. The Greeks who were there got a double blessing in that they got to see and hear Jesus and they also got to hear God speak. As God spoke, He verified that He would honor the ones who served Jesus! What a blessing! Is not the Greeks' request the same that we make in our lives? I'm sure that it is the same because God has made us to seek and find Jesus in our hearts. Thank you, God!

MAY 14
SCRIPTURE: JOHN 1:23 (TEV)

"John answered by quoting the Prophet Isaiah: 'I am the voice of someone shouting in the desert: make a straight path for the Lord to travel.'"

Just as the scripture states, the Lord wants "a straight road to travel."

As the Lord created us in His word with instructions to make a straight road to travel, it is implied that we too should travel a straight road in our daily living. But, we often drift off the straightway in our lives. A definition of drift; an instant of being carried away by currents of water, air, or thoughts. We can easily be found drifting away from Jesus. We are prone to drift as if a boat on the water.

A seagoing vessel requires these fixtures if it is to successfully reach its destination. It needs a captain, power, an anchor, a rudder, and a course. Compare these to our straightway travel in life:

> A captain—God
> A source of power—the Holy Spirit
> An anchor—biblical foundation
> A rudder—Jesus Christ, and
> A course—a conscious acceptance of Jesus and a determined choice to follow His way

Make your choice for living on the straight course listed above. Our part is to keep our eyes on the goal, which is a Christ-like life.

MAY 15
SCRIPTURE: JEREMIAH 29:11–14 (TEV)

"For surely I know the plans I have for you, says the Lord, plans for your welfare and not for harm, to give you a future with hope. Then when you call upon me and come and pray to me, I will hear you. When you search for me, you will find me; if you see me with all your heart, I will let you find me, says the Lord."

God is speaking to His people through a letter from Jeremiah, who writes to the Israelites exiled in Babylon.

If you ever wonder what God knows about you, read the 139th Psalm, which states in the seventh verse, "Where can I go from your spirit?" God states that His plans are for your welfare and not for harm, and I believe that every believer should keep that hope in their heart. Remember, in verse 12, these three promises are made by God: "When you call upon me, you come to me and you pray to me." Then he adds this assurance: "I will hear you!" A most significant word from God when he makes this statement in verse 14: "I will let you find me, says the Lord." Believers should rest in that knowledge.

MAY 16
SCRIPTURE: I CORINTHIANS 1:21–22
(READ 18–31) (TEV)

"For God in His wisdom made it impossible for people to know Him by means of their own wisdom. But for those whom God has called…this message is Christ, who is the power of God and the wisdom of God."

God's wisdom is possessed by Jesus! What then should we learn and know about Jesus? In our world today, does Jesus Christ still matter to our society? Does God's word about His son matter to us? Does our relationship with Jesus really put us right with God? Just what can we know and say that is so special about Jesus? Our society needs to know, we corporately need to know, and we individually need to know. Spiritually, we cannot know those knowing and experiencing Jesus Christ. What then can Jesus do for me? In relationship with Jesus, it has been said that "Jesus shifts my past, shares my present, and shapes my future." We know if we believe the Bible, then Jesus' word is truth! John 5:24 states "I am telling you the truth—whoever hears my word and believes in Him (God) who sent me, has eternal life. He will not be judged, but has already passed from death to life." That is what makes Jesus special and believable.

MAY 17
SCRIPTURE: PHILIPPIANS 4:8-9 (TEV)

"May you always be joyful in your union with the Lord. I say it again, rejoice." "In conclusion, my brothers, fill your minds with those things that are good and that deserve praise: things that are true, noble, right, pure, lovely and honorable."

To be a positive person spiritually, we must continue to be involved in those attitudes and activities that prevent our "rusting out" from inside. To move you in that direction, practice these functions:

> Reading the Bible
> Accepting answered prayers
> Joining group prayers
> Relating to other Christians
> Listening to sermons and literature

Be a positive Christian. Attend church faithfully. Go with God and He will go with you!

MAY 18
SCRIPTURE: JOHN 5:24 (TEV)

"I am the truth: who ever hears my words and believes in Him who sent me has eternal life. We will not be judged, but has already passed from death to life."

The last three words in the sentence above are so powerful that it is sometimes very hard to understand. Apparently, there are three stages of our departing from this earth. Dying…death…life eternal. We will all die one day! We will all be dead, as death will encompass us. However, this scripture above gives us the good news that we will not remain in this state of death, if you have had an experience and believe in Jesus, believe in His word, and believe in God. This scripture states that at the time of accepting Jesus as our Savior we (without Jesus) in our life will not pass into eternal life!

Is your future life ready for the future? The closing sentence in the Book of Matthew is the hallmark for Christian life. Jesus tells His disciples upon His resurrection, "And I will be with you always, to the end of the age!" That means that Christians are safe for ascension into eternal life! Praise God!

MAY 19
SCRIPTURE: GENESIS 12:1-2 (NRSV)

"Now the Lord said to Abram, go from your country and your kindred and your Father's house to the land that I will show you. I will make of you a great nation, and I will bless you, and make your name great, so that you will be a blessing."

A blessing, spiritually, is a gift bestowed by God. Most of us have probably heard a "blessing" most of the time before our meals. Simply stated, a blessing before a meal is a reverent request by someone at the table for God to bless our food and to give thanks to our Lord for the food. For a number of years, I have heard very often people in the South say to me or someone else, "Have a blessed day!" I'm sure that you have heard that also. I just accept the blessing and feel good about the person who has expressed the words. Those words are such motivating words to me; such as the above biblical expression from God to Abram, words I never get tired of hearing: "God bless you!" These three words are awesome, full of God's power. You see, when God blesses, it has a two-point meaning to the person receiving it. Look back at the scripture (for today's reading). God says to Abram, "I will bless you" so that "you will be a blessing." These statements from the Lord are not a mystery that require great study. Just move from your agenda to God's agenda. Be a blessing!

MAY 20
SCRIPTURE: GENESIS 50:20 (NRSV)

"Joseph said to brothers, 'Do not be afraid! Even though you intended to do harm to me, God intended it for good. In order to preserve a numerous people, as He is doing today.'"

Joseph said to his brothers, I cannot change your intentions but God can! How many times has God intervened in your life and changed the possibility of evil acts or thoughts into the certainty of His good? I would expect, as in my case, many times daily. God demonstrates His own love toward us in Romans 5:8: "in that while we were still sinners Christ died for us." How else can we frame the crucifixion except by God's own love for us? We can't, but God can!

MAY 21
SCRIPTURE: ISAIAH 41:8 (NRSV)

"But you Israel, my servant, Jacob, whom I have chosen is the offspring of Abram, my friend."

About friends, I found this statement from poet Claude Mermet that stands out: "Friends are like melons; let me tell you why: to find a good one, you must try one hundred." You can probably identify with that notion! Do you wonder if God has ever felt that way about us? The scripture above names the only time in the Old Testament that God referred to a named person as His friend. However, in the New Testament, Jesus (John 15:15) makes this statement to the disciples: "No longer do I call you servants.... But I have called you friends."

MAY 22
SCRIPTURE: REVELATION 22:12 (TEV)

"'Listen,' says Jesus. 'I am coming soon! I will bring my rewards with me, to give to each one according to what He has done. I am the first and the last, the beginning and the end.'"

My emphasis on this scripture is the phrase "'Listen,' says Jesus." Jesus told His disciples twice in chapter 22 to "Listen." Apparently, the disciples had as much trouble listening as we do today. We all know that the art of listening is not as easy as it might seem. Listening to God is several times harder because He does not speak to us audibly. So, is it impossible to listen to God? Certainly not. For God speaks to us when we are sensitive to His word and actions found in the Bible.

The Bible is our greatest source of relating to Him. However, upon simply reading His word sometimes does not make complete sense; i.e., Matthew 10:34 states, "He who loses his life for my sake will find it." Simply stated, the Lord speaks...we trust! The Lord provides us strength...we respond! Lord, as we speak to you through worship, let us listen and then respond to you.

MAY 23
SCRIPTURE: PSALM 107:1–2 (TEV)

"Give thanks to the Lord, because He is good; His love is eternal! Repeat these words in praise to the Lord all you whom He has saved."

Sometimes we feel as though all is hopeless. But trouble can lead us to depend on God as we cry to Him for help. We should praise Him for the good He has done. Then we understand that God can bring good out of trouble because our afflictions strengthen our faith. Those who have never really suffered may not appreciate God as much as those who have matured under hardship. Those who have experienced God's work have been hardened by the fire of mishap or tragedy.

If you have experienced great trials, you have the potential for great praise. Such were the people in Psalm 107. This chapter might well be referred to as a song of souls set free, because of their being freed from seventy years of captivity in Babylon. This chapter is a call for thanksgiving.

MAY 24
SCRIPTURE: MATTHEW 18:20 (TEV)

"For where two or three come together in my name, I am there with them."

For fifteen years, before becoming a minister, I served as the social worker at our local hospital.

Since being more freed up by the Lord over the past several years, I have found that people in the hospital have requested that I pray for them. At first, my response was to tell them that I would say a prayer for them. Then one day I gave a lady my standard reply and started to leave the room. But my reply was not enough for her. I could see the desire in her eyes and I could feel the urge in my heart. I somehow knew that God wanted me to pray for her right there in her room, right then, at that moment. This would be a new experience for me. Maybe, just maybe, I could do that. She held up a frail, boney hand toward me and I held it. Suddenly, I started praying, heartfelt rather than from the head, and the words just flowed from my mouth. Her smile and words of appreciation told me that something special had occurred right there in that room between us—the little lady, the Lord, and me. I left the room that afternoon thanking Him that I had been able to offer prayers on her behalf.

The next morning, I learned that the lady had died during the night. Since that time, I have never hesitated to pray for anyone who requests such, especially if they are in the hospital.

MAY 25
SCRIPTURE: JEREMIAH 29:10–11 (NRSV)

"For thus says the Lord: Only when Babylon's seventy years are completed will I visit you, and I will fulfill to you my promise and bring you back to this place (Jerusalem)." "For surely I know the plans I have for you."

Have you ever been at a place where you were given a map of that place you wanted to tour or visit? The map may have had a red arrow marking "You are here!" In a way, that may have seemed foolish because you knew where you were. But the indicator helped you to find your way in that particular situation. The above scripture indicates that Jeremiah is reminding that those captured Israelites, who were in Babylon, would return to their homeland as He had promised. The people's capture and their seventy-year-long stay were a result of the Israelites' disobedience. But remember, our God is a faithful God, and He still loved them. He still wanted them to continue their lives even after such an adjustment…so much so that He vows to keep His promise and return them back to Jerusalem. So in your life, where do you find yourself spiritually? Are "you there," somewhere lost? Or are "you here," saved by the grace of God through His son, Jesus Christ? May you be "here" in God's safe keeping!

MAY 26
SCRIPTURE: ISAIAH 43:2 (TEV)

"When you pass through the waters, I will be with you; and through the rivers, they shall not overwhelm you."

One fall my wife had a small poster made with this verse of scripture written in beautiful calligraphy. She gave it to her sister as a gift for her birthday in March. Both of them agreed that this was one of their favorite Bible verses...so it was a gift given with love and accepted with love. Her sister hung it high on her wall, above the door frame in her dressing room. That same year at Eastertime, the city of Jackson was flooded by the worst flood on record. Water covered the roofs of many homes during the flood and many homes were ruined and/or destroyed.

The sister's home had eight feet of water in the interior of the house. Most all their possessions were either washed away or rendered useless by the flood waters. When the waters receded and the family went into their demolished house, the murky water marks were visible on all the walls in the house. As they went from room to room surveying the damage and agonizing the loss of personal items, they were overwhelmed with a sense of loss. You can imagine the feeling of awe when they entered the master bedroom and saw only one undamaged item in the entire house. Yes, still hanging, undisturbed by the flood waters of the mighty Pearl River, the calligraphy poster was still mounted on the wall, untouched by the flood water. Indeed, they had passed through the waters, and God's promise, "They shall not overwhelm you," remained true!

MAY 27
SCRIPTURE: GENESIS 3:11–13 (TEV)

"God asked, did you get the fruit that I told you not to eat? The man answered, the woman you put there with me gave me the fruit and I ate it. The Lord God asked the woman, why did you do this? She then realized, the snake tricked me into eating it."

And from this scripture, we see the beginning of the "blame game." Adam blames God: "The woman you put here with me gave me the fruit." God knew where the woman came from, but Adam wanted to blame God. Then the woman told God, "The snake tricked me into eating it." So the pattern of the blame game began early with humankind! We also know the blame game is played in our world this very day. Blame, Blame, Blame!

Our perception of success is often our primary basis for evaluating others. And condemnation of others then becomes a powerful, destructive force that may communicated, "I'll make you sorry for what you did!" The blame game causes us to assign blame for virtually every failure or error made by others. Sometimes we blame others to make us look or feel better. However, we are not licensed by God to punish or blame others for their mistakes. Rather our response should be love, affirmation, and compassionate correction when possible. And remember, the best reply is to just say, "I'm sorry!"

MAY 28
SCRIPTURE: 2 CORINTHIANS 5:17–18 (NRSV)

"So if anyone is in Christ, there is a new creation; everything old has passed away; see, everything has become new. All this is from God, who reconciled us to Himself through Christ, and has given us the ministry of reconciliation."

This scripture means two things: 1) we are reconciled (brought back) to God through Jesus, and 2) God has given us the ministry of reconciliation. Reconciled, humanly speaking, means to re-establish friendship or relations with another. Spiritually speaking, it means bringing back humankind to God Almighty. The "today's English version" of the Bible uses these words for the above scripture: "All this is done by God, who through Christ changed us from enemies into His friends and gave us the task of making others His friends also." So then, we become an ambassador for the Lord. We become friend-makers for God. In becoming these friend-makers for the Lord, we must do "Jesus' work;" to know Him as our Savior, to accept Him, to obey Him, and to follow Him. God is already everywhere. But the Lord does not enter into our lives unless he is invited. We sometimes start off with great expectations, but when they are not met, we give up. We need to live always aware of Christ in us, so that we reflect Jesus and His love. Let's think of ourselves as mirrors of Jesus.

MAY 29
SCRIPTURE: ROMANS 8:23 AND 26–27 (TEV)

"But it is not just creation alone which groans; we who have the spirit as the first of God's gifts also groan within ourselves as we wait for God…to set our whole being free. The spirit also comes to help us, weak as we are. For we do not know how we ought to pray; the spirit himself pleads with God for us in groans that words cannot express."

To groan means to utter a deep, prolonged sound indicative of pain, grief, or another source of annoyance or joy. Regardless of the cause, it is a release of frustration that may or may not be heard by others. Some of the most assuring words in scripture are these: "For nothing shall be able to separate us from the love of God which is in Christ Jesus our Lord." We can add to this assurance the fact that verse 34 of Romans speaks of Jesus' concern for us in the following words: "Christ Jesus who died, or rather, who was raised to life and is at the right side of God, pleading with Him for us." Bless you, God, that in your plan of salvation for us you gave us a pleading Jesus and a groaning Holy Spirit to care for us.

MAY 30
SCRIPTURE: PSALM 103:1–2 (NRSV)

"Bless the Lord, O my soul, and all that is within me. Bless His Holy name. Bless the Lord, O my soul."

How many of us say "bless the lord" in our prayers or other spiritual times of joy and thanksgiving? We seem to mostly ask the Lord to bless us! But in the 103rd Psalm, David blesses the Lord at least seven times in that chapter. You will note that David begins and ends with the same words of blessings to the Lord. Because of this, the chapter has sometimes been referred to as a "sandwich" Psalm. David knew and had experienced goodness and therefore he wrote this Psalm as a song of thanksgiving. In fact, one writer suggested that chapter may have been sung as a song in early worship of God.

After requesting blessing to be upon God for so many blessings bestowed upon His creation, David finally calls upon all of nature to bless God! We need to bless God more often in our prayers and times of spiritual significance in our lives. Bless the Lord, O my soul!

MAY 31
SCRIPTURE: LUKE 6:36–38 (THE MESSAGE)

"I tell you, love your enemies. Help and give without expecting a return. You'll never—I promise—regret it. Live out this God created identity the way our Father lives toward us, generously and graciously, even when we're at our worst. Our Father is kind; you be kind."

Anytime you show kindness to anyone, with Jesus' love as your basic motivation, you are pleasing God and the recipient of your actions, words, or deeds. Kindness is not against the law. One of God's truly effective workers filled with His kindness was Mother Teresa. One of her famous quotes was this: "Three things in human life are important; First, to be kind; Second, to be kind; Third, to be kind." Kindness can be shown in so many ways—in your home, in relationships with others, in your community, in your church, and even toward your enemy. So you see, even today in our hurry-up world, kindness can be shown and it is still not against the law!

JUNE 1
SCRIPTURE: MATTHEW 8:23–25 (TEV)

"Jesus got into a boat, and His disciples went with Him. Suddenly a fierce storm hit the lake, and the boat was in danger of sinking. But Jesus was asleep. The disciples went to Him and woke Him up: 'Save us, Lord!' they said. 'We are about to die!'"

As you read the Bible, it is obvious that the emotional responses of most people are much the same as we are today. The feeling of despair is sometimes so strong that we are almost overwhelmed. We don't know which way to go or what to do, much as the disciples when in danger (they thought) of the boat sinking. The word "despair" means to lose all hope or confidence. The hopelessness of despair sometimes leads us to desperation in our actions, words, and feelings. In his book *How Prayer Shapes Ministry*, John Biersdorf coins an interesting phrase that he calls "Holy despair." He further defines Holy despair as despair that "comes at the end of ourselves and opens us to something beyond ourselves."

The Israelites were in a state of "Holy despair" when escaping from the Egyptians, for they faced the Red Sea with no means of crossing the waters. They had reached the end of themselves. Holy despair gripped the people. But God became the something beyond themselves. He provided a parting of the sea. and the Israelites walked on dry land to the other side. Their collective lives were saved. They had just experienced "Holy despair." After being saved, they responded with "Holy rejoicing."

JUNE 2
SCRIPTURE: JAMES 3:17 (TEV)

"But the wisdom from above is pure first of all; it is also peaceful, gentle, and friendly; it is full of compassion and produces a harvest of good deeds; it is free from prejudice and hypocrisy."

The life of Tom Lacy fleshed out this passage of scripture for me, especially this phrase "full of compassion and produces a harvest of good deeds." A number of our church members went to his missionary assignment in Belize and worked side by side with him. His purpose was to introduce God and to improve the lives of people living in humble surroundings. They were deep in poverty, but rich in spirit because of His power and love demonstrated through Tom and his family. He introduced the living God to many, many Belizean natives who lived within a twenty-mile radius of his base of operation. Tom was many things to his people…a priest, a physician, an authority figure, a companion, an advisor, a coworker, and a parent. He delivered and he did it with love and compassion.

After visiting and working with him and seeing the gross poverty and lack of physical resources, the most amazing aspect of his work was how the many harvests ever came about. To the person who considers only things like electricity, power equipment, medical supplies, or concrete mixers, Tom didn't have a chance. But for those who know about Christ, about prayer, about sacrifice, about compassion, about commitment, and about fellow travelers, they know why Tom's life produced a harvest of good deeds.

JUNE 3
SCRIPTURE: GENESIS 18:19 (NRSV)

"I have chosen Abraham, that he may charge his children and his household, after him, to keep the way of the Lord by doing righteousness and justice."

"The Way" appears over five hundred times in the Bible. It is used both in a physical and spiritual fashion to indicate direction. Spiritually speaking, the Bible uses the word "way" to point us in the Lord's way. Genesis says to us, "The way of the Lord is doing righteousness and justice." In Psalms 5:8, the psalmist requests of the Lord, "make your way straight before me." These uses of "the way" in the Old Testament establishes the very foundation for the spiritual way that God expects His believers as to how they should live their lives. In the New Testament, Jesus tells Thomas, "I am the way, and the truth, and the life. No one comes to the Father except through me." Jesus really and truly is "the way!"

JUNE 4
SCRIPTURE: 2 PETER 1:12–13 (NRSV)

"Therefore, I intend to keep on reminding you of these things, though you know them already and are established in the truth that has come to you. I think it right, as long as I am in this body, to refresh your memory."

To remember means "to bring back to mind by an effort, to recall." Memory is a gift from God. One we may have taken for granted most of our lives until we start to grow older. We are reminded to remember each time we share Holy Communion. In fact, the statement of Jesus, "Do this in remembrance of me," is often inscribed on the church altar. Most of what the people of biblical times had to remember was relayed to them by word of mouth, so that remembering was essential to the worship of God. Notice this phrase in the twelfth verse of the cited scripture above, "to keep on reminding you of these things." Peter lists these things in an "effort to support your faith." The list is presented in a building block fashion and they include these virtues: goodness, knowledge, self-control, endurance, Godliness, and mutual affection with love. Then Peter adds, "These will keep you from being ineffective and unfruitful in the knowledge of our Lord Jesus Christ." And so, there it is! We go to church each week to worship God…and to refresh our memories of the eternal love of the Trinity through God, the Father, Jesus, the Son, and the Holy Spirit, so that we do not become ineffective and unfruitful in the knowledge of the Lord.

JUNE 5
SCRIPTURE: GALATIANS 5:22–23 (TEV)

"The spirit produces love, joy, peace, patience, kindness, goodness, faithfulness, humility and self-control."

Self-control is a lifetime issue that requires more than we, individually, can conquer. The Bible speaks to this issue on a number of occasions. Paul speaks of self-control in 1 Corinthians 9:25 when he uses athletes as an illustration. He states, "every athlete in training submits to strict disciplines, in order to be crowned with a wreath that will not last: but we do it for One that will last forever." The athlete develops mostly in the area of physical discipline, but as Paul suggests, "the one that will last forever" is spiritual self-control. For Christ-like living we mostly develop self-control in these areas: mental discipline, moral discipline, and social discipline. Self-control is necessary in all areas. Seek God's spirit for help!

JUNE 6
SCRIPTURE: MATTHEW 28:18–19 (NRSV)

"And Jesus came and said to them (the disciples), all authority in Heaven and on earth has been given to me. Go therefore and make disciples of all nations."

Jesus told the disciples to be witnesses to the world. That commandment still is required of believers today, with our world being much larger than it was during the time of Jesus. The idea of making believers may seem just too much for us to handle. But as individuals, we should consider our world as being our area of living our daily lives. With this in mind, it is entirely within our reach and to obey the business of being a witness to the world. At times, we as Christians so identify with the world that our lives can hardly be distinguished from that of a new Christian. Our character, growing out of our relationship of faith in the Lord, makes an outstanding witness of salvation. We as believers become salespeople for God and His church. It has been said that faith lives or dies not by what goes on within the church, but by what, as a result of the church, goes on outside the church. Our witness to the world involves telling our story. We can do this!

JUNE 7
SCRIPTURE: JAMES 3:1 (THE MESSAGE)

"Do you want to be counted wise, to build a reputation for wisdom? Here's what you do. Live well! Live wisely, live humbly."

I once preached a sermon with the title "Two-Word Guidelines." I also searched other scriptures and found many two-word guidelines that offer to us great advice and suggestions for living a life that is pleasing to God. All of these suggestions could really be summed up with this two-word offering: "Christ-like." In living Christ-like lives, we cultivate and maintain the Lord's desire for us to have a love-relationship with Him! Here is a short list of two-word phrases that have real significance for believers:

> Get Serious
> Ask God
> Give In
> Clean Up
> Get Down
> Let God

Using these simple two-word phrases in developing your own testimony of your spiritual journey can be very effective. You don't have to be a gifted speaker with long, authoritative words. Get serious and start your preparation!

JUNE 8
SCRIPTURE: JAMES 1:19 (THE MESSAGE)

"Post this at all the intersections; Dear Friends: lead with your ears, follow up with your tongue, and let anger straggle along in the rear."

Straggle is a word that I was not totally familiar with, so I had to look it up. It means "to fall behind in unplanned disarray or disorder." That's a good use of the word because it needs to be behind all other emotions that we use in our words and actions. Often we as believers talk the talk and forget that we are to exhibit our words in our lives. Those who speak with flowery words seem to pale when their acts look like thorn bushes. We preachers sometimes act like those bushes. The key issue is not what is said or preached, but what is done in our actions.

James 21:21 (NRSV) tells us to rid ourselves of sordidness and wickedness and "welcome with meekness the implanted word (of God) that has the power to save your soul." The subheading in the (NRSV) Bible for this scripture today is hearing and doing. In order to do these things, we must lead with our ears, follow with our tongues, and let anger straggle extremely in the rear of our speech and actions.

JUNE 9
SCRIPTURE: DEUTERONOMY 8:2 (NRSV)

"Remember the long way that the Lord your God has led you these forty years in the wilderness, in order to humble you, testing you to know what was in your heart, whether or not you would keep His commandments."

Have you ever traveled with a child/children and got about a mile from your starting point and the child starts asking, "Are we there yet?" And how many times do you have to answer? I started thinking, I wonder how many times Moses had been asked that same question during the forty years of wandering in wilderness, going to the "Promised Land"? They apparently were not lost; God was testing them according to the above scripture. The Lord was leading them. In the book *Jayber Crow* by Wendell Berry, his main character states: "Often I have not known where I was going until I was already there. I am an ignorant pilgrim crossing a dark valley. And yet for a long time, looking back, I have been unable to shake off the feeling that I have been led!" Have you ever experienced that feeling? Are we there yet? As believers, we are working on getting there, where we find peace in one another's love, compassion, and forgiveness; these are God's gifts to humankind. Our faith keeps us moving in that direction!

JUNE 10
SCRIPTURE: 2 CORINTHIANS 10:1 AND 4 (NRSV)

"I myself, Paul, appeal to you by the meekness and gentleness of Christ. For the weapons of our warfare are not merely human, but they have divine power to destroy strongholds."

Paul states that Christian warfare should be characterized by these two elements: meekness and gentleness. He is dealing with a difficult period in his relation with the church in Corinth. He further states he does not want to show boldness but deal with the people of the church with the meekness and gentleness as displayed and taught by Jesus. Meekness and gentleness are sometimes used interchangeably. (For this devotion I will use the word *gentleness*). Aristotle defined the word as "the correct means between being too angry and being never angry at all." It describes that person who is never angry at anyone's wrong, insult, or injury they may receive, but who is capable of righteous anger when they see others hurt, injured, or insulted. When not seen in its true context, the word *gentleness* sometimes is offensive to male persons. Gentleness, at times, presents the idea associated with weakness, and compromise. The real meaning is that of power under control and strength, balanced with tenderness. Jesus was a model of righteous indignation! But, he demonstrated that tenderness by gentleness.

JUNE 11
SCRIPTURE: EXODUS 17:5–6 (NRSV)

"The Lord said to Moses, I will be standing there in front of you on the rock at Horeb. Strike the rock, and water will come out of it, so that the people may drink. Moses did so, in the sight of the elders of Israel."

For such a great miracle, Moses' job was very simple. The group of God's people who were wandering in the wilderness found that they were in a water-less area and quarreled with Moses and blamed him for even leading them from Egyptian captivity. When Moses followed God's instructions, all Moses had to do was strike a rock with his walking stick! What a demonstration of God's concern and power!

The faithful God that we as believers worship wants what is best for us, and sometimes He responds in almost unbelievable acts of compassion. But, then He is God! Jesus reminds us in scripture this statement: "apart from me, you can do nothing." It may be as simple as Moses' part in this miracle: Just "strike the rock!"

JUNE 12
SCRIPTURE: ACTS 1:8 (NRSV)

"But you will receive power when the Holy Spirit has come upon you; and you will be my witnesses in Jerusalem, in all of Judea and Samaria, and to the ends of the earth."

You could say that life as a Christian boils down to these five actions on our part:

> To worship God
> To love and accept Jesus
> To do unto others
> To be His witness
> To care for His creation

Perhaps the most difficult of these tasks presented to us is to be His witness. "Be my witness." God is talking to you and me. He is talking to His precious humankind, the part of His creation for whom He said in Genesis, "I am well pleased." As Christians, we know this very day to whom this command is intended. Throughout the Christian history, this command has been successful in carrying the word to the world. God expects and depends on this "torch of His desire" to be ever passed on to the unsaved.

Dear friend, that torch has been passed on to us as the witness to share within our frame of reference. Let us not be found passing the buck on to others to do our Christian duty! There are limitless excuses that we can find to negate our responsibility that God commands us to do. All you have to do is to tell your story of your personal experience with Jesus Christ. God does the rest! Be His witness.

JUNE 13
SCRIPTURE: PSALM 95:1–2 (TEV)

"Come, let us praise the Lord! Let us sing for joy to God, who protects us! Let us come before Him with thanksgiving and sing joyful songs of praise."

We are filled with expressions of joy and thanksgiving because at some point in our lives, we surrender our lives to the Lord and were saved by the grace of God. He is our God and we have no doubt about it! We are the people He cares for and our response should be that of the psalmist who states, "Come, let us bow down and worship Him." We should be a thankful people, called to God by the inner voice of the Lord who created us and cares for us. In each of our lives, God wants us to look up, to look around, and to look forward so that we will count our blessings!

JUNE 14
SCRIPTURE: LUKE 6:47 (NRSV)

"Jesus said, 'I will show you what someone is like who comes to me, hear my words, and acts on them.'"

I want to call your attention to Jesus' statement quoted above, which He says requires a response from one who is seeking Him. All three elements in this instruction have action verbs that require initiative by the person. The verbs are to come, to hear, and to act. A positive response to the actions ensure one of approval and acceptance from Jesus. He compares the follow-through on these three actions to the man who builds his house on an indestructible foundation. The person who builds his house on ground without a strong foundation is in danger of losing his house. Jesus makes this statement about the house: "Great was the ruin of that house!" It is when we "come to Jesus" in repentance, and confession, and accept His forgiveness, that we turn to Christ-like living. God, according to Isaiah, said, "Here I am; I will help you!"

JUNE 15
SCRIPTURE: GALATIANS 5:1 (TEV)

"Freedom is what we have, Christ has set us free! Stand, then, as free people, and do not allow yourselves to become slaves again."

Consider the debt we owe this very day to God and country and to each other. No matter what else may be demanding our time and our attention, let us take time to remember and give thanks for the unpayable debt that we owe to God! God has given us every good blessing we enjoy in our lives. Isaiah 5:2-7 tells of a friend who expected a fine crop from his vineyard. He waited for the grapes to ripen, but every grape was sour. Israel is the vineyard and the people are the grapes. This is what the Lord said He would do: "I will take away the hedge around it. Break down the wall that protects it, and let wild animals eat it and trample it down." Verse 8 then states the Lord's response to His people's actions: "You are doomed!" This story teaches us that God has a right to expect love, worship, honor, and obedience from us, the cornerstone of His creation.

Unfortunately, many of us are like the people in biblical times. We show little gratitude for our many blessings given to us by God. We often break His moral laws. When we behave in this manner, God has a right to act in judgment! History reveals that whenever a nation ignores God and rejects His word, it reaps a bitter harvest! We often say that the USA is "one nation under God." Is that a truth that is growing dimmer for our country?

JUNE 16
SCRIPTURE: MATTHEW 5:16 (TEV)

"Let your light shine before people, so that they will see the good things you do and praise your Father in Heaven."

In our "doing good things," we give people a chance to see our work. However, the most important benefit that is demonstrated is that our action shows how God is working in and through us. We thus become spiritual conductors! A conductor is an instrument that transfers an action from one object or person to another. Just as an electric cord transfers electricity from a plug-in to a television set, it really doesn't matter what you call the action, it is what you say and do!

We as believers need to increase our words and actions that reflects God's love and grace to others. Some may refer to this process as "witnessing" or sharing your story (testimony). These actions on our part may be difficult for us to do. But think of your words as making us ambassadors for the Lord. 2 Corinthians 5:19 states that "God has committed to us the word of reconciliation." Now then, we are ambassadors for Christ. Learn to testify!

JUNE 17
SCRIPTURE: SELECTED

We profit from the grace of God in so many ways. We have to remember that God loves us whether we want Him to or not. In the New Testament, we become God's children through Jesus by adoption. Let me list six ways in which we are blessed by God's free grace:

> You have been adopted (Romans 8:15)
> You are a member of His Kingdom (Colossians 1:13)
> You are beyond condemnation (John 5:24)
> You will never be abandoned (John 6:37)
> You have access to God at any moment (Matthew 18:19)
> You have an imperishable inheritance (Matthew 6:14)

Think on these gifts and join with the songwriter who wrote "Amazing Grace."

JUNE 18
SCRIPTURE: ROMANS 5:2 (NRSV)

"Through our Lord Jesus Christ we have access by faith into this grace in which we stand and rejoice in hope of the glory of God."

The world does not understand where or why as Christians we know that we are safe in God's grace: The above scripture tells us that grace provides the place in which we stand spiritually. This is the point, "What you see is determined by where you stand." The Christian values on which believers stand are invisible to the world. My wife's friend once told her, "My mother said to always keep an invisible means of support in back of you!" For me that invisible support is God's love, mercy, and grace. While these gifts from God are invisible to the eye, the meaning of these characteristics can be fleshed out by believers in their words, deeds, and actions. As Christians we stand on invisible means of support that are gifts from God to share with others. Take your stand with God!

JUNE 19
SCRIPTURE: ISAIAH 65:1 (TEV)

"The Lord said, 'I was ready to answer my people's prayers…I was always ready to answer, "Here I am; I will help you."'"

If we could truly learn to forget self and rely on God's promise in this verse, how much more freed up we would be to praise Him and to serve others! God does not put conditions on His answers or His help. Not only does He say, "I was ready," He says, "I was ALWAYS ready." Can you imagine that, always ready? Not just when you are at your best, not just on Sunday at worship, but when misery is paramount, when hurt envelops your being…He is ready.

Somehow in attempting to accomplish the American way of pulling ourselves up by our bootstraps, we either are successful and boast of our knowledge, expertise, and independence, or we fail and slump into a state of failure and depression. In neither case do we turn to God, usually because of our own ego. Rather we forget to give God praise for our success or we blame Him for our failure. Both responses on our part reflect spiritual weakness because God is excluded. He does not want to be left out. The word "always," in this verse, means that He is omnipresent in our lives, by *His* will. We may choose to remain apart from Him but the exclusion is of our making, not His.

How much clearer can God emphasize His readiness than to state without even being asked, "Here I am; I will help you."

JUNE 20
SCRIPTURE: LUKE 8:43–48 (NRSV)

"As He went, the crowds pressed in on Jesus. Now there was a woman who had been suffering from a disease for twelve years; no one could help her. She came up behind Him and touched the fringe of His clothes and immediately she was healed."

The trip made by Jesus was not unlike much of His travels by foot. Large groups of people gathered around Jesus as they walked with Him. The Bible tells us, "The crowds almost crushed Him!" We read these facts regarding the woman. She went through three emotional states: desperation, determination, and deliverance. The desperation can be seen in the length of her illness without a cure. The determination can be seen in the woman's act of coming up behind Jesus and touching the fringe of His clothing. The deliverance is seen in Jesus' healing remark to the woman: "Daughter, your faith has made you well; go in peace." What better reward could we receive than experience the "touch of Jesus" and become daughters and sons of God?

JUNE 21
SCRIPTURE: JOHN 1:38-39 (NRSV)

"When Jesus turned and saw them following, He said to them, 'What are you looking for? They said to Him, Rabbi (which means teacher), where are you staying? He said to them, 'Come and see.'"

Upon inquiry from the followers of John the Baptist, Jesus issued the simplest yet one of the most compelling of invitations, which completely changed their lives—and the lives of people over the next two thousand years. That invitation was simply this: "come and see." The Bible tells us that the two spent the rest of the day with Jesus. We do not know what Jesus and the two men discussed that afternoon. In fact, the Bible does not indicate their discussion. But as the result of that occasion, these men became the first two disciples of Jesus. That three-word invitation from Jesus is still just as significant to the people of our time. At some point in our lives, we responded to that invitation from Jesus. The Bible can tell you what others have seen when Jesus called. Most were changed in their hearts, their spirits, and their behavior. We need to consider these two questions when we consider our spiritual lives. Who is this Jesus? And what is our relationship with Him? During this time of consideration and self-examination is the time to see and experience Jesus' grace.

JUNE 22
SCRIPTURE: 1 TIMOTHY 2:3–4 AND ACTS 4:12 (TEV)

"It pleases God our Savior, who wants everyone to be saved and to come to know the truth." (1 Timothy 2:3-4) "Salvation is to be found through Jesus alone; in all the world there is no one else whom God has given who can save us." (Acts 4:12)

To rational persons, what do these two scriptures mean? It is God's desire for us to be saved and not to be condemned. God is standing with open arms, just like the Father of this prodigal son, to welcome us into His arms. Listen to this statement, "The will of God will not take you to a place where the grace of God will not protect you!" What a wonderful interpretation of God's love for us. The purpose of our lives is far greater than your own personal fulfillment, your peace of mind, or even your happiness. If you wonder about your purposes, then we should begin with God. You were born by His purpose and for His purpose. Focusing on ourselves will never reveal our life's purpose. The Bible tells us in Job 12:10, "It is God who directs the lives of His creatures; everyone's life is in His power." Until we understand that, life will never make sense.

JUNE 23
SCRIPTURE: HEBREWS 4:12–13 (TEV)

"The word of God is alive and active, sharper than any double-edged sword."

I once saw a bumper sticker on a car that read, "Read the Bible, it will scare the hell out of you." The above scripture states that God's word is "alive and active." Then the writer gives us several reasons for the word being alive and active:

> Sharper than a double-edge sword
> Divides soul from spirit
> Divides joints from marrow
> Judges thoughts and intentions of the heart
> Sees all creatures, and
> Makes us all naked before Him

These functions of the word of God are to bare to the eyes of the one to whom we must "render an account of ourselves." This accounting of ourselves will be disastrous if we are not reconciled to God!

JUNE 24
SCRIPTURE: PSALMS 66:16–20 (TEV)

"Come and listen, all who honor God, and I will tell you what He has done for me. I cried to Him for help; I praised Him with songs. God has indeed heard me; He has listened to my prayer. I praise God, because He did not reject my prayer or keep back His constant love from me."

For most people, the acronym ASAP means "as soon as possible." But for Christians it can also mean "always say a prayer." You may be facing a problem that leaves you with a feeling of helplessness. We know that God is all powerful; we can go to Him in prayer. It has been said, "Prayer is the deepest, dearest, honest, strongest way we have of trusting God and loving one another. In prayer, we just call to the depths of God's love from the depths of our lives." Teach us, Lord, as we pray to have believing hearts. You want what is best for us even when we do not understand your response. Still, help us to continue to have believing hearts.

JUNE 25
SCRIPTURE: EPHESIANS 2:4–5 (TEV)

"God's mercy is so abundant, and His love for us is so great that while we were spiritually dead in our disobedience, He brought us to life with Christ. It is by God's grace that you have been saved."

If we aren't careful, we can be spiritually "looking good on the outside, but far from God in our hearts." He is most interested and concerned with what is in our hearts. He wants our heart and minds free of greed, dishonesty, hatred, pride, and selfishness that can be found in the deep shadows of our hearts. That is why we need to get right with God before it becomes our outward words, deeds, and/or actions. Rev. Albert Barnes wrote, "There cannot be conceived a stronger expression to denote the urgency of God in the conversion and salvation of humankind than that of God's grace." God's grace must be received inside our being before it can be demonstrated outside.

JUNE 26
SCRIPTURE: ACTS 3:19–20 (NRSV)

"Repent therefore, and turn to God so that your sins may be wiped out, so that time of refreshing may come from the presence of the Lord."

Several years ago one of the car manufacturing companies had a recall for automobiles of a certain kind that had faulty parts and offered to replace the part through their recall offer. It was a free offer! However, despite the risk of serious injury, thirty percent of the car owners never responded! In the scripture above, Paul calls for us to "repent and turn to God" for his forgiveness. He is saying in effect that God gives us a "recall notice." Unlike a defect found in automobiles, the moral defect found in humankind is not the creator's fault! Genesis 1:31 tells us that God makes everything "very good." But the sins of humankind ruined the relationship with God. Repenting of our sins is necessary to be put right with God. In the Presbyterian Church, PC USA, the definition of repentance is this: "Repentance is namely a sincere turning to God and all good, and earnestly turning from the Devil and all evil." This is what God's recall does for us and His notice is free!

JUNE 27
SCRIPTURE: MARK 2:10–12 (NRSV)

"But so that you may know that the Son of man has authority on earth to forgive sins." He said to the paralytic, 'I say to you, stand up, take your mat and go to your home.' And he stood up, and immediately took the mat and went out before all of the people."

This scripture demonstrates two basic elements of Jesus' characteristics, love and forgiveness. Both elements are greatly needed in our society today, rather than the doom and gloom we see and hear about daily. Both unrest and fighting seem to be present in all parts of the globe. Forgiveness reminds me of the return of the prodigal son. Remember how the son practices his apology? "Father, I have sinned against heaven and against you. I no longer deserve to be called your son." But remember the Father's response! He does not even give the son a chance to apologize! The Father returned his son's request for forgiveness with a spontaneous forgiveness. What a great lesson for us to imitate in our lives.

JUNE 28
SCRIPTURE: JOHN 1:14 (TEV)

"The word became a human being and, full of grace and truth, lived among us. We saw His glory, the glory which He received as the Father's only son."

John the disciple was an eyewitness to Jesus' ministry and was known as "the one Jesus loved." Apparently, John wrote his book so that readers might believe that Jesus is the son of God. In the book, John listed six miracles or signs to prove the power of God. You may read each in the following chapters of the Book of John:

Chapter 2, Jesus turns the water into wine
Chapter 4, the healing of an official's son
Chapter 5, the healing of the sick
Chapter 6, the feeding of the five thousand people
Chapter 6, walking on water, and
Chapter 9, healing of a blind man

Notice John's symbolic use of things that would be known by most of the people; i.e., water, bread, light, grapevine, etc. The use of these things from everyday life were illustrations of God's gifts to the people so that Jesus is accepted as the Way, the Truth, and the Life.

JUNE 29
SCRIPTURE: JOEL 1:17–18 (TEV)

"Have pity on your people, Lord. Do not let other nations despise us and mock us by saying, 'Where is your God?' Then the Lord showed concern for His land; He had mercy on His people."

The Book of Joel describes a terrible invasion of locusts and a devastating drought in Palestine during time of the Persian Empire. He sees that a time will come when the Lord will punish His people with a great attack of the land by swarming locusts. He describes the attacks of the locusts in graphic detail! "They attack like warriors; they climb the walls like soldiers; they swarm through defenses; they rush against the city; they run over the walls; they climb up the houses and go in through the windows like thieves." (Joel 2:7-9). The Lord puts out a call to the people: "Repent sincerely and return to me with fasting and weeping, and mourning. Come back to the Lord your God. He is kind and full of mercy." Then the Lord had mercy, had concern for people and His land, and removed the locusts. The prayers and repentant actions of the people brought about a change in God's plans. Could we not benefit from such prayers and repentant prayers in our time?

JUNE 30
SCRIPTURE: I TIMOTHY 1:13-14 (TEV)

"God was merciful to me because I did not yet have faith and did not know what I was doing. And our Lord poured out His abundant grace on me and gave me the faith and love which are ours in union with Christ Jesus."

Being empty and being filled are processes that require a motivated action to fulfill a desired result. To be empty means to be void of content (created by pouring out or never having had content). Filling means to occupy a desired space with content. Let's consider these two actions from a spiritual viewpoint. Paul's two statements in the above scripture presents to us a spiritual condition that changed his life. Paul, as we know, was a man who persecuted believers with a passion to end the Jesus movement. He was feared by believers because of his anger toward them. We could say that he was empty of God's spirit, heart, and soul. But God's plan for Paul took a drastic turn when he encountered Jesus. He was filled with God's grace that made a change in his life. He went from a persecutor to a recruiter. God changed him completely even when Paul states "even though in the past I spoke evil of the Lord and persecuted and insulted Him." God still used Paul to spread the word. God, according to Paul, "poured out his abundant grace on Him. God in effect said to Paul, as He had said to Isaiah (65:1), "Here I am, I will help you!" Thank God He still says that to us when we are spiritually empty.

JULY 1
SCRIPTURE: JOHN 15:14–15 (NRSV)

"This is my commandment, that you love one another as I have loved you. No one has greater love than this, to lay down one's life for one's friends. You are my friends…I have called you friends because I have made known to you everything that I have heard from my Father."

One of God's greatest gifts for His precious humankind was to have a system of support for every person. That system includes the Trinity, families, and friends. A friend is defined as a person attached to another by affection and/or regard. The Bible describes many interesting statements and stories about friends. Proverbs 17:17 states, "A friend loves at all times." John 15:15 states, "Jesus said, 'no longer do I call you servants…but I have called you friends.'" The Lord wants you and me to be friend-makers for God. Friends love us because of who we are. You are you! And you are loved!

JULY 2
SCRIPTURE: MATTHEW 4:23 AND 5:1–2 (TEV)

"Jesus went all over Galilee, teaching in the synagogues, preaching the Good News about the kingdom, and healing people who had all kinds of disease and sickness. Jesus saw the crowds and went up a hill, where He sat down. His disciples gathered around Him, and He began to teach them."

This scripture relates to us how to be "fishermen of men." Jesus uses three very effective methods of educating His disciples. He was about these three methods during His three-year ministry. They still have educational value for us today; teaching, preaching, and healing. Jesus' first major teaching was to the crowds who gathered for the "Sermon on the Mount." He used common, everyday objects that were known by most people of His day.

Jesus used examples that were easily understood. The amazing fact is that He continues to use these same techniques with you. He has enough confidence in you and love of you, to reflect that same love to those with whom you have daily contact. He wants you to be part of His mission to tell the world who He is. He delights in asking you to join Him!

JULY 3
SCRIPTURE: MATTHEW 10:39 (THE MESSAGE)

"If your first concern is to look after yourself, you'll never find yourself. But if you forget about yourself and look to Me, you'll find both yourself and Me."

Until we experience Jesus, our natural inclination is to "get all we can!" The rule of the spiritual person should be to "give all you can!" The difference, of course, is the difference between the meaning of the two words *get* and *give*. To "get" means to come to have possession, use, or enjoy an object. To "give" means to present voluntarily and without expecting reward or compensation. In the spiritual realm, only that which we give away will we keep forever. John the Baptist said, "Less of me and more of Jesus." The concept of the above scripture could be more clearly understood by thinking of the game of dominoes. How so, you may ask? You win by losing. You have to win by losing all your dominoes first. Whoever plays all their dominoes first wins the game. It's not like other games where the winner gets the most runs, points, or scores. In dominoes, you try to lose to win, or put another way, you have to extend energy to gain energy. It is more difficult to put into action in our spiritual experiences. Jesus taught this concept as He was preparing the disciples before sending them out to preach. In Matthew 10, Jesus said, "If you forget about yourself and look to me, you'll find both yourself and me!" Think about that! That's a win-win situation!

JULY 4
SCRIPTURE: JOHN 6: 37–38 (TEV)

"Everyone whom my Father gives me will come to me. I will never turn away anyone who comes to me, because I have come down from heaven to do not my own will but the will of Him who sent me."

We need to be very careful in our judgment of others. We are most often prone to look for the bad, place blame, or otherwise castigate, sometimes even our families and/or our friends. I have a bad habit of attempting to seek motive in the actions of others. Having found a motive, I then proceed to pass judgment. If a person is an alcoholic, he's no good; if a person is poor, he's lazy; and on and on I am tempted to go. Perhaps some of you are guilty of this type of thinking and know what I am talking about. If so, you need to join me in turning to the Master to see his example.

Look at the people He served, for whom He felt compassion, and those whom He healed. They were prostitutes, tax collectors, prisoners, poor people, the down and out, the outcasts of the communities. But you see, He says, "I will never turn away anyone who comes to me." The secret seems to be in this action phrase: "who comes to me." I would add, in a state of repentance.

Gracious Jesus, He even accepted *me*!

JULY 5
SCRIPTURE: JAMES 4:7–8 (NRSV)

"Submit yourself therefore to God. Resist the Devil, and he will flee from you. Draw near to God, and He will draw near to you."

The devil is such a deceiver! He takes such pain in attempting to disrupt your actions, especially if they are directed to God, goodness, or compassion to others. He tries to tempt you in every way that he thinks will alter your Christ-like actions or words or behaviors. In Job's case, the devil took all of his possessions, property, and children. But Job remained positive toward the Lord. The devil was so sure of his powers, he tempted Jesus on three occasions in the fourth chapter of Matthew, verses 1-11. Notice Jesus' responses to the devil after each temptation. Jesus quoted from the scriptures each time: "But it is written! Worship the Lord your God, and serve only Him." Just imagine Jesus could have dealt with the devil in any way that you could bring to mind. But Jesus responded with the reality of the power of God as appears in the scriptures. And look at the devil's response. Verse 11 makes this statement, "Then the devil left Jesus, and suddenly angels came and waited on Jesus." Score these temptations, Jesus—3 and the devil—0! Look again at the above scripture; James tells us to "resist the Devil and he (devil) will flee from you." This last quote points out how very weak and cowardly the devil is. Follow James' progressions when tempted by the devil: 1) submit to God, 2) resist the devil and He will flee, (3) draw near to God, and (4) God will draw near to you. Such a great model of dealing with temptation. The Message version of the Bible states, "Yell a loud NO to the Devil and watch him scamper!"

JULY 6
SCRIPTURE: MICAH 7:18 (TEV)

"There is no other God like you, O Lord; you forgive the sins of your people."

For Christians, one of the most assuring statements in the Bible is the scripture above. That assurance offers a deeper meaning to our life's journey. Love will be more enhancing, forgiveness will be more real, our hearts will be more revealing, because our Lord will fully extend to us His love, mercy, and grace, even into eternity! God wants only what's best for us. His gift to us of free will guarantees them when we chose His way. Good choices bring about good consequences. The Lord "does not want from us the best calves, thousands of sheep, endless streams of olive oil, or our firstborn child—no! The Lord "wants us to do what is right, to show constant love, and to live in humble fellowship with Him."

JULY 7
SCRIPTURE: MATTHEW 16:18 (NRSV)

"And I tell you, you are Peter, and on this rock I will build my church, and the gates of hades will not prevail against it."

Jesus said, "I will build my church." During these days of so much controversy about denominations, views, teaching, and interpretation of doctrines, it may be good to look again at the church as scripture explains it. Not from a denominational point of view, but from a spiritual view. You can look to the Books of Acts to see how Christianity grew immediately after Jesus' crucifixion. Jesus calls the creation of the church "His church." It was built upon Christ and His teachings, the rock of ages. The church is the body of Christ. It is to bring Him glory! We may ask in our troubled times: How secure is the church? Based on Jesus' declaration, "the gates of hades will not prevail against it!" We can be totally assured that the church is secure. The church will stand until Jesus comes again!

JULY 8
SCRIPTURE: GALATIANS 1: 6–7 (TEV)

"I am surprised at you! In no time at all you are deserting the one who called you by the grace of Christ, and are accepting another gospel, actually, there is no other gospel."

Martin Luther once profoundly proclaimed, "Here I stand. I can do no other." It has been written of Martin Luther that "he stood; for the world alone, for Christ alone, for grace alone, for faith alone, and in Christ alone. To the Glory of God alone." In some ways, our times remind us of the people in biblical times during the days described in the Book of Judges. The nation of Israel had no leader and chaos existed among the people. The last sentence in the Book of Judges reads: "There was no king in Israel at that time. Everyone did what he pleased." Have we as a people, as believers, returned in our spiritual journey to the days of king-less Israel? Some even believe that Jesus is not the only way to gain salvation! That sounds like "another gospel." But the word of God is the only true gospel." As believers of the Lord Jesus Christ, we believe that He is the only way to gain salvation. It has been said, "You have to stand up for something or you will fall for anything." Stand up for Jesus, now!

JULY 9
SCRIPTURE: HEBREWS 12:14 (TEV)

"Try to be at peace with everyone, and try to live a Holy life, because no one will see the Lord without it."

One of the greatest challenges that we have is to allow God to free up our lives from our own selves. Through His grace, love, and mercy he can free my life so that I have the freedom to be me. This freedom to be me has frightening implications because it means review of my raw self and all the sin therein. The Lord knows that we cannot totally be at peace with everyone. Perhaps that's why this verse repeats "try" two times. But with His help, the freedom to be me provides the opportunity to be at peace with Him, myself, and others.

It is almost beyond my belief system that He wants to be seen in me! He believes enough in me that He gives me the precious privilege of being His representative.

JULY 10
SCRIPTURE: 2 CORINTHIANS 5:17 (NRSV)

"If any is in Christ, He is a new creation; old things have passed away; behold, all things have become new."

In the process of swapping or trading objects, the concept of "as is" becomes an essential reality. "As is" means that one accepts the item without benefit of the usual protection of money-back guarantee, contract, etc. The owner accepts responsibility that the object will continue to function. It constitutes an acceptance on the basis of "purchaser beware." Jesus accepted His disciples on an "as is" basis. Mark 2:12 tells us, "Jesus went back again to the shore of Lake Galilee. As He walked along, He saw a tax collector, Levi, sitting in his office. Jesus said to him, "Follow me! Levi got up and followed Him." You see, Jesus accepted a tax collector even though he was not a person well-liked by his fellow citizens. He may even have been despised by most of the people. Jesus takes the same initiative of acceptance with each of us when we are brought into His way, just "as is!" He looks into our hearts and sees the potential that God gave us. He then trades our sinful nature for His acceptance of us as a possible believer. He chooses us on an "as is" basis! He accepts us without a guarantee, without a return if not fully satisfied, without a negotiated contract. Jesus simply and unconditionally accepts us "as is!"

JULY 11
SCRIPTURE: MARK 6:30–32 (NRSV)

"The disciples gathered around Jesus, and told Him all they had done and taught. He said to them, 'Come away to a deserted place all by yourselves and rest a while! For many were coming and going, and they had no leisure even to eat.' And they went away in the boat to a deserted place by themselves."

The disciples seemed in a rush all the time…coming and going, doing and being there. Do you ever feel that you are at the end of your road? Maybe down to the knot at the end of the rope? Perhaps you need a good dose of just plain old solitude. Not solitude to dwell on your problems or troubles, but time to be with the Lord. Try to find time each day or so when you can turn off the business of the world and turn to the Lord. Find a quiet, special place where you can meet God to meditate on His word, to evaluate your circumstances, and rededicate your efforts. Jesus knew the limitations of humanity and the need for constant restoration. Jesus went to God many times during His life. If it was good enough for Jesus, it is good enough for us.

JULY 12
SCRIPTURE: PSALM 25:4-7 (NRSV)

"Make me to know your ways, O Lord; teach me your paths. Lead me in your truth, and teach me, for you are the God of my salvation. For you I wait all day long. Be mindful of your mercy, O Lord, and of your steadfast love, for they have been from of old. Do not remember the sins of my youth or my transgressions. According to your steadfast love remember me, for your goodness' sake, O Lord!"

What is the psalmist seeking in all these requests? Make me, lead me, remember me, teach me. This person seems to be in serious distress. He desires salvation! Why does he/she make these requests to God? Look at the motives for these requests. The psalmist is in reality saying, "I have no hope except in you!" The psalmist also recognizes the sins in his life, even from youth. He knows that he is a sinner. He has met God in his heart and realizes that he is unworthy.

Don't we seek salvation and forgiveness of sin? Haven't we met God in our hearts and know our sins? Then, the psalmist requests that God forgive him through His mercy, His everlasting love, and kindness. People are watching us in most all our activities. We have a big job to do for God. The hymn writer Peter Sholtes perhaps expressed it best in his song: "They will know we are Christians by our Love!"

JULY 13
SCRIPTURE: PSALM 56:13 (TEV)

"So I walk in the presence of God, in the light that shines on the living."

We know of the physical light the God brought into the world upon creation when He spoke these words: "Let there be light and there was light." God also created in humankind a spiritual light. And in the Book of Isaiah proclaims, "I the Lord, will be your eternal light." Does that eternal light that God speaks of in the Old Testament still shine for us today? You bet your life it does! That eternal light is now present in Jesus Christ, who reflects it into us upon an experience with Him. In John 8:12, Jesus says, "I am the light of the world. Whoever follows me will have the light of life." The Lord wants us to practice right living in His light like the people we know or have known, are people who put others before themselves. Their lights can be seen in the life of their community, in others, and in you. When needs exist, they light up lives so that people can move from darkness into the Lord's light.

JULY 14
SCRIPTURE: HABAKKUK 1:1-3 (TEV)

"O Lord, how long must I call for help before you listen, before you save us from violence? Why do you make me see such trouble? How can you stand to look on such wrongdoings? Destruction and violence are all around me, and there is fighting and quarreling everywhere."

These are the words of the Prophet at the end of the Babylonians' rule over the people of Israel. He was deeply disturbed by the violence of cruel people. Habakkuk could have well been writing about our world today! Our nation today is experiencing wars, hunger, drugs, crime, attacks on churches, and on and on! The Prophet continues, "Look at the nations and see! Be astonished! Be astonished!" These things happen when people live in a fallen world. And we are in that same fallen world...just at a different time!

Julia Ward Howe's defiant song, "Battle Hymn of the Republic," expresses our nation's voices and intentions to battle the evil forces of our nation and the world. "God is marching on!" In His own time, the Lord will cease to be tolerant of the people of the world and will right the wrongs of all times. God has always been "marching on" in the history of the world, magnificently illustrated in His creation of the world, the lives of His people, the leaders of the nations, and the believers of Jesus Christ. In our own times and lives, God is still marching on. Be prepared, persistent and pray!

JULY 15
SCRIPTURE: ISAIAH 42:6-7 (NRSV)

"I am the Lord, I have called you in righteousness, I have taken you by the hand and kept you; I have given you as a covenant to the people, a light to the nations to open the eyes that are blind, to bring out the prisoners from the dungeon, from the prison those who sit in darkness."

The Lord in the above scripture told the Prophet, "I have called you!" The Lord called to Adam and Eve, to Abraham, to Israel, and to many others in the Bible. God has called to the humankind since the beginning of creation. Basically, God's calls for servanthood, obedience, and righteousness. Some have answered His call; others have not answered. A call from the Lord is a summons with an invitation. Part of Christ's mission was to demonstrate God's righteousness and bring light to the whole world. Through Christ we all have an opportunity to be servants for the Lord. How are we equipped by God to be His servants? The Lord wants believers to exhibit the kingdom of Heaven in our daily lives by involvement in missions (foreign and or local), in evangelism, in demonstration of our life in your world. Listen for a call to you from the Lord.

JULY 16
SCRIPTURE: PSALM 71:17–18 (TEV)

"You have taught me ever since I was young, and I still tell of your wonderful acts. Now that I am old and my hair is gray, do not abandon me, O God! Be with me while I proclaim your power and might to all generations to come."

The psalmist in the above scripture is speaking to God at the time that is particularly personal to me as I have just turned eighty-one years and am almost totally gray on the head. Growing old has at least two advantages: 1) a time viewed in our senior years for retirement benefits, a time of freedom to do nothing, or a time to purchase discounts, or; 2) accept the senior years as a great time of spiritual blessings to pass on to others. I read of a man who was 102 years old. When asked how he faced life at his advanced age, he replied, "Every morning when I get out of bed I make one of two choices. To be happy or to be unhappy." Then he said, "I always choose to be happy!" One of God's greatest gifts to us is the blessing of choice. We all know that every situation does not offer us a choice. Some situations come to us with consequences already set, offering no opportunity for choice. A recent country song offers us this advice: "When the music plays, I hope you choose to dance, rather than to sit it out!" Establish that as your mindset! Choose to dance!

JULY 17
SCRIPTURE: ROMANS 12:2 (NRSV)

"Do not be conformed to this world, but be transformed by the renewing of your minds, so that you may discern what is the will of God—what is good and acceptable and perfect."

We are transformed by renewing our minds by the message of God's grace found in His word. Spiritual growth is the process of replacing lies and myths with the truth. The truth will set you free. Renewing our minds involves being re-educated and redirected in our efforts to have an obedient heart. We must abide in God's word, study His word, and respond to His word. There are more copies of the Bible now than during any other age in history. For most of the over two thousand years of Christianity, only priests could read the Bible. Today, millions of people can successfully read and understand the word of God. However, many prefer the daily newspaper and leave God's word to hearsay or less.

We cannot watch TV or use the computer four to five hours a day, read and study the Bible five to ten minutes per day, and expect to grow spiritually. A Bible on the shelf is of little use to you. Feeding on God's word should be one of our daily priorities. Jesus called it "abiding." He said, "If you abide in my word, then you are truly disciples of mine." We need to acknowledge our sins, accept forgiveness from God, and adjust to renewing our minds. Just do it!

JULY 18
SCRIPTURE: LUKE 4:1 (TEV)

"Jesus returned from the Jordan full of the Holy Spirit and was led by the spirit into the desert."

This scripture shows that He was led into the desert where He was tempted by the devil. Then immediately after the temptation, verse 14 states, "Then Jesus returned to Galilee, and the power of the Holy Spirit was with Him." Both these verses point to Jesus' source of driving force as the Holy Spirit. Many forces drive our lives and our direction in life. The verb "drives" means to guide, to control, or to direct. These types of "drives" are probably conducted by us daily. But consider this: What is the driving force in your life? More importantly, what is the driving force in your spiritual life? In addition to Jesus' driving force of the Holy Spirit, other sources appear throughout the New Testament—those being scripture, prayer, and relationships of love. We could never go wrong by using Jesus' models!

JULY 19
SCRIPTURE: JOHN 3:29-30 (NRSV)

"This is how my own happiness is made complete. He (Jesus) must become more important while I become less important."

John the Baptist was involved in ministry before Jesus started, and in this scripture John's disciples were reporting to Him, "Well He (Jesus) is baptizing now, and everyone is going to Him!" John reminded His disciples that he had told them, "I am not the Messiah, but I have been sent ahead of Him; and He (Jesus) must become more important while I become less important." In this manner, John further states that his happiness will be made more complete. Earlier when John baptized Jesus, God had told John, "the one on whom the dove (spirit) landed would be the one who would baptize with the Holy Spirit." Perhaps by John's statement His disciples felt anger, frustration, or challenge for leadership in this new religious movement. John himself had been preaching and even drawing crowds and baptizing. But God had spoken to John and he knew that Jesus was the Son of God. John apparently had been happy to be the messenger, but his happiness was made complete by the coming of Jesus and His ministry.

JULY 20
SCRIPTURE: JEREMIAH 17:5-7 (NRSV)

"Thus says the Lord; cursed are those who trust in mere mortals and make mere flesh their strength, whose hearts turn away from the Lord. They shall be like a shrub in the desert, and shall not see when relief comes. They shall live in the parched places of the wilderness, in an uninhabited salt land. Blessed are those who trust in the Lord, whose trust is the Lord."

The dilemma of humankind began in the Garden of Eden and continues to our time even though God has offered us redemption through Jesus Christ. We of this age have not improved in our actions toward God or others. God's people continue to sin even when we know of: God's law, the Prophets of God, the Son of God, and a history of God's miracles found in the Bible.

It would appear that humankind's dilemma is a matter of our hearts, "whose hearts turn away from the Lord." When a person's ability to reason is misdirected, their will is at odds with the will of God and the heart turns from God and His way. Still loving us in spite of our sins, God provides us the opportunity to return to Him in the act of repentance. How thankful we are that He did!

JULY 21
SCRIPTURE: 1 PETER 1:34 (TEV)

"Let us give thanks to the God and Father of our Lord Jesus Christ! Because of His great mercy He gave us new life by raising Jesus Christ from death. This fills us with a living hope."

A definition of hope is the feeling that what is wanted can be had. Ed Howe stated, "We should not expect something for nothing, but we all do; and we call it hope." We hope for many things in our lifetime; spiritual hope is an ongoing process for believers. In the Old Testament only the people of the nation of Israel were referred as God's chosen people. But through Christ, all believers become God's chosen people. We are called into a living hope of eternal life, which begins when we accept Jesus as our personal Savior.

JULY 22
SCRIPTURE: EPHESIANS 2:10 (TEV)

"God has made us what we are, and in union with Christ Jesus He has created us for a life of good deeds, which He has already prepared for us to do."

God didn't verbally tell us what we are to do in life as a vocation. Most of us prepared for that through experience, schooling, and hard knocks. Through prayer, training, and good fortune, most of us have become productive. Regardless of our vocation, God has declared that He has made us in union with Jesus for good works. He expects us to do good works in every walk of our life. Not only has God made us for good works, He has already prepared those works beforehand and those activities are to become our way of life. He has already prepared them. All we have to do is "just do them!" What then are the good works for us to do? Really, the things that He wants us to do are the things we want done unto us! There are too many to list but you know them. I suggest that you put these three items in your approach to the tasks God wants you to do: prayer, deeds, and action. James tells us, "The prayer of the righteous is powerful and effective."

JULY 23
SCRIPTURE: 2 CORINTHIANS 5:17–18 AND 20B (TEV)

"When anyone is joined to Christ, He is a new being; the old is gone, the new has come. All this is done by God, who through Christ changed us from enemies into His friends and gave us the task of making others His friends also. We plead on Christ's behalf; let God change you from enemies into His friends."

I recently read this amazing statement: "You are as close to God as you choose to be." Like friendship, you must work at developing that relationship with God. James 4:8 states, "Draw close to God and God will draw close to you." This is not a difficult concept to experience. Just think of a developing romantic relationship and how the two grow in love for each other. But this type of friendship goes only so far. The friendship such as this is only a fore-taste of our love extended to us through the grace of God. Again, 2 Corinthians, fifth chapter reminds us, "God is making all mankind His friends through Christ." When we understand God's love through Jesus, we know that God uses everything good in our lives. Don't overlook in the above scripture that "God gave us the task of making others His friends also!"

JULY 24
SCRIPTURE: COLOSSIANS 2:1-3 (TEV)

"Let me tell you how hard I have worked for you.... I do this in order that we may be filled with courage and may be drawn together in love, and so have the full wealth of assurance which true understanding brings. In this way, they will know God's secret, which is Christ Himself. He is the key that opens all the hidden treasures of God's wisdom and knowledge."

Paul is saying in the above scripture that Jesus is the key to God's secrets regarding wisdom and knowledge. Further He states that, "Jesus is the key that opens the treasures of God's secret." The example of "a key" to describe God's desire to opening and closing of His treasures is a point well made by Paul. There are several meanings of the word "key" in the dictionary. I like this one: "something that affords a means to achieve something else." God's treasure for believers is to be reconciled to Him after humankind's fall from His grace. So, God gives us the gift of Jesus to be God's instrument for that reconciliation! Jesus is there by the means, or the key, to our redemption and salvation. Check the keys in your possession and be sure that you have the key that opens God's treasures.

JULY 25
SCRIPTURE: HEBREWS 12:1B–2 (TEV)

"Let us run with determination the race that is before us. Let us keep our eyes fixed on Jesus, on whom our faith depends from beginning to end. He did not give up because of the cross! On the contrary, because of the joy that was waiting for Him, He thought nothing of the disgrace of dying on the cross, and He is now seated at the right side of God's throne."

The writer of the above scripture advises us to run to escape the sinful situations that we often find ourselves involved in. We don't need to move out with a wait-till-tomorrow attitude. No! This scripture indicates that we should run from sin and then run toward Jesus with our focus on Him. Why? Because our faith depends on Him, from beginning to end. The writer states to run with determination. At all times during the race of determination, we should keep our eyes fixed on Jesus. Still stay focused on Jesus when we meet with trial, temptations, and sorrows. When we keep our eyes fixed on Jesus, we experience that; Jesus rules our lives, the Holy Spirit is with us, and we enjoy close fellowship with God and others.

JULY 26
SCRIPTURE: JOB 42:1–5 (TEV)

"I talked about things I did not understand, about marvels too great for me to know…. Then I knew only what others have told me, but now I have seen You with my own eyes."

> It may have been in days gone by, when questioning God's love, I ceased to try…
>
> And being content with worldly explanation, I simply refused to look toward His creation.
>
> Then I saw the gentle touch of a daughter, with a father slowly dying,
>
> Exhausted from endless effort, but still hoping and trying…
>
> It may have been, in days gone by,
> But then I saw God with my own eye.
>
> Then I experienced the joy of a brother's
> Unselfish sharing, and in him, I saw God caring.
>
> It may have been, in days gone by,
> But then I saw God with my own eye.
>
> Then I looked at the Cross and saw
> Jesus in my stead,
>
> Soul that hurt and body that bled,
> it may have been, in days gone by,
>
> But then I saw God with my own eye.
>
> – by Charles C. Ray

Aren't we just like Job? Before our encounter with the living Christ, we knew Him because of what others told us. But after the encounter, we know Him because we have seen Him with our own eyes…

JULY 27
SCRIPTURE: 2 CORINTHIANS: 4:16–18 (NRSV)

"So we do not lose heart. Even though our outer nature is wasting away, our inner nature is being renewed day by day for this slight momentary affliction is preparing us for an eternal weight of glory beyond all measure, because we look not at what we can see, but at what cannot be seen, for what can be seen is temporary, but what cannot be seen is eternal."

This means that we are living by faith; such is the believer's basis for considering there is a heaven. The Bible tells us a surprising number of things about heaven. For believers, it is the heaven of salvation. No space vehicle can ever be devised to carry us there. This is the true heaven and it can only be gained by the redeemed, not by brain inventions. In John, Jesus told Nicodemus, "A man could not even see this heaven, let alone enter it, unless He was born again." Jesus also taught His disciples to pray, "Our Father who art in Heaven." Jesus was referring to the heaven in which God dwells. Our most desired goal is to be with the trinity in heaven for an eternity.

JULY 28
SCRIPTURE: LUKE 16:19–21 (TEV)

"There was once a rich man who dressed in the most expensive clothes and lived in great luxury every day. There was also a poor man named Lazarus, covered with sores, who used to be brought to the rich man's door, hoping to eat the bits of food that fell from the rich man's table."

Jesus told the story of the rich man and Lazarus to warn the Pharisees (and us) of the danger of wealth. The story does not condemn the rich man just because he was rich. He is condemned purely because he failed to use his wealth in the service of God by concerning himself with the sufferings of his fellow man. A poor man would be likewise condemned if he behaved in the same manner to a brother who was even poorer. However, the Pharisees looked upon wealth as the reward for righteousness. Their religion praised wealth as a coverup for hearts filled with greed. As believers, we do not accept, as the Pharisees did, that plenty is a sign of God's favor and that poverty is a sign of God's judgment. The Pharisees after death were to go to hades. Sometimes our attitude might be, "Who cares?" Do we even believe that there is a hell anymore? Hell is real! While we may not be able to tell where hell is or how to describe hell, we do know that hell is separation from God! The "larger catechism" of the Presbyterian Church states: "The punishment of sin in the world to come is everlasting separation from the comfortable presence of God, and most grievous torments in soul and body. Jesus came to seek and save the lost.

JULY 29
SCRIPTURE: PSALM 92:1–2 (NRSV)

"It is good to give thanks to the Lord, to sing praises to your name, O most high; to declare your steadfast love in the morning, and your faithfulness by night!"

Synonyms for praise include: applause, esteem, exaltation, approval, admiration, tribute, grace, and thanksgiving. There is power in praising God. There are many calls to praise God in the Bible, especially in Psalms. We should be able to enhance our practice of praise to Him! I once read that it is better to praise than to panic! It is better to praise than to be pessimistic! It is better to praise than be problem conscious!

Present-day attitudes of praise are difficult for us to utter because of the world we live in today. Expressions of joy, admiration, and thanksgiving are not immediately called to mind except in unusual circumstances. We seem to be of the mind that the gift of praise is no longer necessary.

When fishing, every cast I make, I am expecting to catch a big fish. Why not? However, faith in Christ enables us to expect and hope for the best in every situation. Therefore, let us be more sensitive to all things worthy of our praise and offer up to our Lord an offering of grateful homage as an act of worship.

JULY 30
SCRIPTURE: GALATIANS 4:16–17 (NRSV)

"Live by the spirit, I say, and do not gratify the desires of the flesh. For what the flesh desires is opposed to the spirit, and what the spirit desires is opposed to the flesh; for these are opposed to each other, to prevent you from doing what you want."

Someone said to me recently that the greatest battle that we as human beings face is the enormous struggle that we have within our very being. This is particularly true for the believer. Paul tells us that the struggle is between our sinful inclinations and the Holy Spirit who lives with us. The "message Bible" explains Paul's dilemma in this fashion, in Romans 7:19-20: "What I don't understand about myself is that I decide one way, but then I act another. Doing things I absolutely despise. So if I can't be trusted to figure out what is best for myself and then do it; it becomes obvious that God's command is necessary. But I need something more!" In Paul's struggles against sin, and consequently our struggles against sin, he seems to have learned these three truths:

1. Knowledge is not the answer. "I do not understand my own actions!"
2. Self-determination in one's own strength does not succeed. Paul found himself involved in sins in ways that were not even attractive to him.
3. Being a Christian does not stamp out all sins and temptations in a person's life. And when we fail, we must realize that sin is stronger than we are. So Paul, in Romans 7:24, asks this gut-wrenching question "Wretched man that I am! Who will rescue me from this body of death?" Paul answered his own questions: "Thanks be to God through Jesus Christ our Lord!"

JULY 31
SCRIPTURE: REVELATION 3:22 AND 4:1 (NRSV)

"Let anyone who has an ear listen to what the spirit is saying to the churches. After this I looked, and there in heaven a door stood open! And the first voice, which I had heard speaking to me like a trumpet, said, 'Come up here....'"

The Lord gives us a personal invitation to our eventual eternal home in the last three words of the above scripture. In fact, the invitation is from Jesus to John: "Come up here!" Reminds me of a story about a country preacher who told the congregation that believers are not exempt from troubles. Sometimes we are surrounded by troubles to the right...to the left...in front...in rear. A very faithful man in the congregation stood up and shouted, "Glory to God, it's always open at the top!" Have you ever received an ordered package of an object wrapped carefully by the manufacturer or sending company? Most instructions on the outside of the package say, "Open at the top!" Following instructions, one finds the contents of the package: packed securely, in orderly fashion, free from damage, and ready for assembly or use. God wants us to live our lives open at the top, so that we are not encumbered by circumstances that box us in... that block us in, every direction. Open at the top so that we can look and pray upward toward heaven with the sure knowledge that we are God's children, ever moving with upward mobility.

AUGUST 1
SCRIPTURE: 1 PETER 5:7 (NRSV)

"Cast all your anxiety on Him, because He cares for you."

No matter what Bible translation, God cares for you! What God means in this scripture is that He wants you to lighten your load and travel light. How much more intimate can God be than for you to be His personal concern? The King James Version of the Bible says this about the above scripture, "He careth for you!" This is the whole message of the Bible. If you get nothing else from this devotion, remember this four-word sentence, "He careth for you." Re-examine who you are: a fallen individual; in bondage to sin; subject to God's Holy judgment. Without God's intervening grace and salvation, we are condemned and lost.

We may place burdens on ourselves or they may be placed upon us by others, or by circumstances beyond our control, but God did not intend for such to happen! When we are burdened, listen to what Jesus said in Matthew 11:28: "Come to me, all you that are weary and are carrying heavy burdens, and I will give you rest." It's like God gives us a safety net, and Jesus Christ is that safety net.

AUGUST 2
SCRIPTURE: LUKE 22:27 (TEV)

"Who is greater: the one who sits down to eat or the one who serves Him? The one who sits down, of course. But, I am among you as one who serves."

Jesus is telling the disciples that He was one who serves others. This concept was totally foreign to their mind-set. They believed that Jesus was the Messiah; however, for them and most of Israel, the Messiah was expected to be like a king or one who will come and physically, politically, and economically rescue the people. He would overcome their enemies and establish peace, justice, and goodwill. For generations, the people of Israel had waited and suffered for the wonderful arrival. The disciples must have thought, and at times said among themselves, why does Jesus continue by words, deeds, and actions to demonstrate and verbalize this business of the Messiah being one who serves? In our culture today, most of us strive for wealth, strong influence, large houses, big cars, accumulations of stocks and bonds…none of which Jesus possessed! But Jesus' purpose and plans were so radical that even His closest associates did not understand. Even today, many people still do not want to operate the "Jesus-fashion." Jesus told His disciples, "whoever wants to be first must place Himself last of all and be the servant of all." How radical!

AUGUST 3
SCRIPTURE: JOHN 15:15–16 (TEV)

"I call you friends, because I have told you everything I heard from my Father. You did not choose me; I chose you and appointed you to go and bear much fruit, the kind of fruit that endures."

One of my former pastors told us that God created all humankind as "divine originals." That seems to be a good appraisal of who we are, divine originals. Like His disciples, Jesus chose us, you and me! He tells us that we are to bear fruit, to be faithful to God, and to love one another. Each of us has been given gifts to accomplish our "ministry." When we respond, it is our choice and not chance that determines our destiny. Max Lucado in one of his books writes that about choice: "Because of Calvary, I'm free to choose. And so I choose love, joy, peace, patience, kindness, goodness, faithfulness, humility and self-control."

These attributes we know as the Fruits of the Spirit are found in Galatians 5:22-23. What do you choose?

AUGUST 4
SCRIPTURE: MATTHEW 23:28 (TEV)

"On the outside you appear good to everybody, but inside you are full of
hypocrisy and sins."

Whatever happened to sin? Do we, today, even recognize or spiritually
acknowledge sin? Have our Christian values become so watered down that
we have few if any Christian absolutes or truths to guide us in our earthly
journey? Do our associates, friends, or peers dictate what is right, what is wrong
instead of relying on Christian teachings? A noted psychiatrist of the twentieth
century wrote that his analysis of the problems of these diagnoses: gloom,
apprehension, depression, and discouragement were caused as a result of sin.
The doctor called for universal recognition of sin as a prevention against self-
destruction. One U.S. church denomination defines sin as a turn from God and
what is good, to a turn to evil and turn to the devil. The word "sin" has almost
disappeared from our vocabulary, but the problem of guilt remains in the hearts
and minds of our people. Repentance, the Bible tells us, removes the guilt of sin
and affords a new life in Jesus Christ.

AUGUST 5
SCRIPTURE: 1 CORINTHIANS 10:13 (NRSV)

"No testing has overtaken you that is not common to everyone. God is faithful, and He will not let you be tested beyond your strength, but with the testing He will also provide the way out so that you may be able to endure it."

We have experienced enough of life to know that God has and will test us. But rest assured, God is faithful and His promises are sure and true. Lest we forget, God does not always light the whole path that we may see clearly, but He usually lights the way for your next step. God's testing helps us to learn to let go of our own fears and trust in Him. A popular theme about the same statement is this: "Let go and let God." Sometimes this is easier said than done. Your testing is not unique to you; God will not allow your test to be beyond your strength. He will provide a way out of your testing; and you will be able to endure the testing. So again, "Let go and let God!"

AUGUST 6
SCRIPTURE: PSALM 16:11 (TEV)

"The Lord will show me the path that leads to life; His presence fills me with joy and brings me pleasure forever."

David in this scripture is telling us that he is experiencing God's presence confidently. Have you ever felt the presence of God? Perhaps, in a particular place or setting, at a specific time, with a special person, or even under the most unusual circumstances. When you least expected it, God's presence came near. It is a most awesome experience! It may be brief, but not without it vibrating your heart and your senses. (Re-examine David's words above). We really do not have to summon God to our side…He is already there!

AUGUST 7
SCRIPTURE: PHILIPPIANS 2:13 (TEV)

"God is always at work in you to make you willing and able to obey His own purpose."

I think that we all have had these special people in our lives who have made a difference for us. Matthew 12:35 is a good reason for this because as is stated, "Good people have good things in their hearts." For me, Jim was one of those "good people." He had a serious disease (of diabetes) and had already had one leg amputated, was totally blind, and was the only white person to live in a black housing project. Over a period of the next two years, he adopted me and my family and we adopted him.

During this time, we learned these facts about Jim:

> He had been raised in a New York Children's Home
> Had no relatives in the South
> Was discharged from military service in Biloxi, Mississippi
> Moved to our town for employment
> We helped him move to an apartment
> Our friends helped with rent, utilities, medical care
> We helped him secure "books on tape"
> We worked out plan for him to fly to New York for one month to visit the Children's Home
> Died of a massive heart attack
> We planned his funeral and his burial in a local cemetery

In our relationship, Jim demonstrated to me, in full fashion, Jesus' command "to love one another." His love for me and my children released in my heart a deep and abiding love for him. That's the way love works! It opens to us the caring heart that God instilled in our lives at birth. Philippians 1:6 tells us this: "I am sure that he who started a good work in you, will carry it on to completion until the day of Christ Jesus." Thank you, Lord, for Jim!

AUGUST 8
SCRIPTURE: JOHN 1:29 (TEV)

"The next day John saw Jesus coming to him and said, 'There is the lamb of God, who takes away the sin of the world.'"

In one of Max Lucado's inspirational writings entitled "Imperfect People," he depicts Jesus as a trash man who meets troubled sinners and suggests that they empty their trash on him. The trash man is willing and able to lift the loads of trash and relieved them of their sins. That is in real life exactly what Jesus does when we have a spiritual experience with Him! We know that Jesus is more than able to rescue us from our sins and shortcomings—from our garbage, as it were. Sometimes the bags of junk almost immobilize us, to the extent that only the Lord can save us. Rev. Lucado's image is of Jesus taking the bags, lifting them over His head, and emptying the refuge on Himself. While I have never really thought of Jesus in the role of a trash man, it does make thoughtful meaning for each of us. But we must remember that Jesus Himself said, "I have come into the world to save sinners!" Praise God!

AUGUST 9
SCRIPTURE: JOB 38:1–3 (TEV)

"Then out of the storm the Lord spoke to Job, 'Who are you to question my wisdom with your ignorant, empty words? Stand up now like a man and answer the questions I ask you.'"

If you have read the Book of Job, you are aware of the unbelievable destructive events that occurred in his life. The scripture tells us God's questions for Job were this: "Who are you to question my wisdom?" And then God asks Job a series of questions. God used Job's ignorance of earth's natural order to reveal Job's ignorance of God's moral order. If Job could not understand God's physical creation, then how could he possibly understand God's mind and character? (Read chapter 38 for God's questions of Job.)

Proverbs 2:6 states, "It is the Lord who gives wisdom." Colossians tells us, "Jesus is the key that opens all the hidden treasures of God's wisdom and knowledge." So I ask you, who are we to question God's wisdom?

AUGUST 10
SCRIPTURE: 1 PETER 1:4 (TEV)

"We look forward to possessing the rich blessings that God keeps for His people. He keeps them for you in heaven, where they cannot decay or spoil or fade away."

This scripture seems to suggest that God has prepared for believers a Holy inheritance that He keeps for His people. It is possible to inherit all types of things from others; i.e., money, physical possessions, property, etc. My brothers and I have traced our family tree back for twelve generations, but try as we may, we could not find any rich relatives from whom we could inherit. My father was not a wealthy man in terms of earthly wealth or things. However, he did leave us intangible values that are more than money could ever buy, like honesty, a solid work ethic, a love of family, a deep love and respect for our mother (and consequently, we have great love and respect for our wives). And so our inheritance from our parents makes us wealthy in Christ-like possessions. A Holy inheritance will be ours in His time and far more marvelous.

AUGUST 11
SCRIPTURE: JOHN 15:8 (TEV)

"My Father's glory is shown by your bearing much fruit; and in this way you become my disciples."

One of the Christians' doctrines indicates, "Man's chief end is to glorify God, and to enjoy Him forever." He created you to be you and me to be me. He made us in His image and He wants us to glorify Him in our journey. Paul says, "Accept each other just as Christ has accepted you; then God will be glorified." Loving other believers has a three-part action; it glorifies God, it benefits others, and it pleases you. Each of us is a divine original; designed by God with gifts, talents, skills, and abilities. But God did not give us these gifts for selfish purposes. He gave us the responsibility of glorifying Him and serving others.

AUGUST 12
SCRIPTURE: MATTHEW 27:22 (NRSV)

"Pilate said to them, 'Then what should I do with Jesus who is called the Messiah?'"

Let's return to the same question of Pilate; the same one that all humankind must not only ask, but more importantly must answer, "What should I do with Jesus?" Those who have had a life-changing experience with the living Lord Jesus Christ answer the question by an act of surrender to Him. You know that person by their actions, their words, their compassion because their actions and deeds come from their hearts. They have been redeemed by "God's riches at Christ's expense," which is an acronym for "Grace."

AUGUST 13
SCRIPTURE: JOHN 15:11 (TEV)

"Jesus said, 'I have told you this (just as I have obeyed my Father's commands and remain in His love) so that my joy may be in you and that your joy may be complete.'"

When I find myself in circumstances beyond my control; in troubles that I have not created; in doubts that tend to immobilize; caught up in selfish attitudes; tempted by immoral thoughts or actions, I turn to Jesus in my prayers, seeking that joy I had earlier experienced. The same Jesus and the same joy that I experienced when I surrendered my life to Jesus. And as I recalled that time as I prayed, that same joy returned in my heart. My actions and attitude about my life returned to a faithful God who loved me still. I felt as if I heard, as the disciples did, when Jesus ascended into heaven, "and I will be with you always, to the end of the age." Can there possibly be any greater source for our joy?

AUGUST 14
SCRIPTURE: MATTHEW 4:10 (TEV)

"Worship the Lord your God and serve only Him."

I once read a story of a goldsmith who sat on the floor of his workroom waiting for the gold to purify before he made the precious ore into valuable objects of art. Someone asked him, "How do you know how long to sit and wait?" The goldsmith replied, "When I can see my face in it!" Perhaps, that is why God waits for the duration of our temptation. He wants to see the reflection of His own face in our lives. When God sees His reflection in our lives, others will see His reflection in our lives.

AUGUST 15
SCRIPTURE: GENESIS 4:7 (TEV)

"Because you have done evil, sin is crouching at your door. It wants to rule you, but you must overcome it."

The Lord is questioning Cain as to why he is angry at the Lord's acceptance of Abel's offering and rejection of Cain's. The Lord said to Cain, "Sin is lurking at the door. It's desire is for you, but you must master it." (NRSV) Sin is still very present in the world today! However, sin seems not to be seriously considered in our lives. The attitude of "do whatever make you feel good" prevails. We seem to think so highly of ourselves that we either think that we hide sin from God or we just don't care! "So what, everybody is doing it!" Why master it when we can cover it up? The only way for us to master sin is to confess to God and receive and accept His forgiveness!

AUGUST 16
SCRIPTURE: JOEL 2:12–13 (TEV)

"'But even now,' says the Lord, 'repent sincerely and return to me with fasting and weeping and mourning."

God reassures His people though the Prophet Joel with these three words, "But even now!" Right in the mist of all the devastation brought on by the attacks of the army of locusts that almost totally destroyed the nation of Israel. They suffered loss of crops, trees, seeds, bringing about a loss of cattle and sheep! Can the conditions get any worse for the people of Judah? Has their suffering reached the point of no return? Is this to be the end of God's people? Conditions are so terrible for the people that they raise this question: "Who will survive it?" But God intervenes, stating, "But even now; repent and return to me." Do we see how long, how patient, and how much He loves His people, including you and me? The Lord remains faithful and He offers us choices, even when we are not worthy! Even in our lowest, loneliest, darkest hour, the Lord says to us, "But even now!"

AUGUST 17
SCRIPTURE: 11 CORINTHIANS 10:1 (NRSV)

"I myself, Paul, appeal to you by the meekness and gentleness of Christ; I who am humbled when face to face with you, but bold toward you when I am away."

Paul's second letter to the Corinthians was written during a difficult period in His relation with the church at Corinth. Even in the times of difficulty, Paul writes that Christian warfare should be characterized by these two approaches, meekness and gentleness. These two words are used interchangeably, so I will use gentleness in this devotion. Gentleness has been defined as "the correct means between being too angry and never being angry at all." It describes the person who is never angered at personal wrong, insult, or verbal injury but is angry when they see others hurt, injured, or insulted. This type of anger is sometimes referred to as righteous indignation. Gentleness is usually thought of in one of two ways—either weakness, passivity, or compromise, or as power under control, producing strength, balance, or tenderness. Paul's approach was to "appeal to the church members by meekness and gentleness." Paul's method is more effective in bringing about reconciliation.

AUGUST 18
SCRIPTURE: PSALM 103:5 (NRSV)

"The Lord satisfies you with good as long as you live so that your youth is renewed like the eagle's."

We are never called to retire and just coast on home to heaven! In Psalm 92:14, David states, "They shall still bear fruit in old age; they shall be fresh and flourishing." I have heard this about growing older: "Old age is a matter of mind over matter. If you don't mind, it doesn't matter." Apparently, John Kelley practiced "mind over matter." He ran in the Boston Marathon fifty-eight times, the last one when he was eighty-four years old. He died at age ninety-six. Even when we are no longer physically active, the Lord expects us to be active in our prayer life and in quiet service. Remember, the accumulation of years of older life nor the lack of years in youth seem to be any hindrance to your living. Some people are old at twenty; others are young at seventy. Gray hair, wrinkled skin, poor balance, and loss of hearing are not indicators of old age; they just mean that we have been here a long time. Regardless of our age, keep in touch with the Lord in your daily lives, so He "will satisfy you with good as long as you live."

AUGUST 19
SCRIPTURE: JOHN 20:28–29 (NRSV)

"'My Lord and my God!' So Jesus said to Thomas, 'You needed the eyes of sight to make you believe; but the days will come when men will see with the eye of faith, and will believe.'"

Look closely at Jesus' statement: "when men will see with the eye of faith, and will believe." What a profound statement that has come true, even to our day. It will remain an eternal proclamation until the end of time. We believe through the eye of faith, without physically seeing through the eye. Thomas' initial response was probably one that we would have announced. Never was the saying "Seeing is believing" more true!

In reality, faith comes by our hearing, studying God's word, and experiencing Jesus Christ. When we do not participate in any of these three actions, faith will not be seen.

AUGUST 20
SCRIPTURE: 1 TIMOTHY 4:8-9 (TEV)

"Physical exercise has some value, but spiritual exercise is valuable in every way, because it promises life both for the present and for the future. This is a true saying to be completely accepted and believed."

Let me start by sharing some sayings that I heard when I was a little boy. I wondered for a long time if they were true sayings:

> "Don't walk under a ladder. It's bad luck."
> "Don't continue down a road if a black cat crosses in front of you. Bad luck."
> "Don't allow anyone to sweep under the chair that you are seated in. You won't get married."
> "Don't leave home without wearing clean underwear. You may have an accident."

I'm sure Paul did not mention any of these sayings to Timothy. However, Paul wanted to reinforce Christian beliefs (sayings) to his young friend and assistant. Paul recognized that Timothy was willing and able to work with newly established church groups. He also needed Paul's advice, consent, and support. Paul is trying to deeply instill in this young evangelist the true word of God. He wants Timothy to be clear and certain about God's word. Let this scripture be a reminder to us of the value of spiritual exercise.

AUGUST 21
SCRIPTURE: HEBREWS 1:1–2 (TEV)

"Now faith is the assurance of things hoped for. The conviction of things not seen. Indeed, by faith our ancestors received approval."

A definition of faith is "an unquestioning belief, specifically in God." Albert Barnes wrote this definition: "Faith states what is the nature of all true faith, and is the only definition of which, is attempted in the scriptures." Scripture lists the realities that we cannot see, but by our faith we feel and act as if they were real. We do not see the trinity, heaven, angels, the redeemed in Glory, the crowns of victory, the harps of praise. But we have faith and we incorporate them into our very lives. They give us reality of our hearts and souls. You see, you must have faith in God to even seek Him. What a witness that bears evidence to the reality of Almighty God.

AUGUST 22
SCRIPTURE: ACTS 3:19-20 (NRSV)

"Repent therefore, and turn to God so that your sins may be wiped out, so that times of refreshing may come from the presence of the Lord."

To repent is like a response from a person who receives a "recall" notice from a manufacturer of a product that has been declared to have a malfunction. The manufacturer then gives the one who purchased the item the right to allow for repair or refusal of same. The manufacturer then responds based on our decision. We can consider a recall of this sort to the call, by God, to repent of our sins and return to Him as taught us through accepting Jesus as our personal Savior. The decisions for our actions are left up to us. They include: to repent, to confess our sins, to accept the Lord's forgiveness, to change our lifestyle to a Christ-like life. This decision of repentance then as the Bible teaches puts us right with God again. Just like He created us to be! Even after repenting, we still offend the Lord by our continued disobedience. He loves us again and again to bring us back to His mercy and love and grace.

AUGUST 23
SCRIPTURE: GALATIANS 5:19–20 (TEV)

"What human nature does is quite plain. It shows itself in immoral, filthy, and indecent actions; in worship of idols and witchcraft."

Somewhere in the living experience, it was learned that one could rid themselves of their surplus goods by exchanging those goods to someone else for their surplus goods. This action is what we call "trading." I remember "trading" marbles when I wanted another boy's certain marble and he wanted a certain one of my marbles. Consequently, we traded marbles and we were both made happy. As long as "trade" functions go smoothly, both parties are satisfied with their new objects. God has a spiritual trading plan for humankind. It involves one giving up their sinful nature and accepting God's forgiving gifts of mercy, grace, and love. His trading plan started when God sent His son, Jesus, as His "object" offer for our sins. Jesus focused on healing, preaching, and teaching. His trademark was the cross, though Jesus Christ allows us to trade those works of the flesh for acceptable behaviors that are reflected in living by the fruit of the spirit. What a trade! All our sins (traded to the Lord) for the fruit of the spirit, which includes "love, joy, peace, patience, kindness, goodness, faithfulness, humility, and self-control." If you have not made the trade, do so today!

AUGUST 24
SCRIPTURE: 1ST CORINTHIANS 1:30 (TEV)

"God has brought you into union with Christ Jesus, and God has made Christ to be our wisdom. By Him we are put right with God; we become God's Holy people and are set free."

You see, the new covenant that God made with His people (including the Gentiles) tells us that He has already "written on our hearts that He is our God and we are His people." It is already there, inscribed on our hearts. Our hearts may be so full of clutter that we never know of God's love and grace that is extended. If you believe the Bible and have accepted Jesus as your Savior, God's laws are engraved on your heart and can never be removed. May people see the reflection of the Lord in our faces and our lives.

AUGUST 25
SCRIPTURE: 2 PETER 1:2 (NRSV)

"May grace and peace be yours in abundance in the knowledge of God and of Jesus our Lord."

Peter is telling us in his salutation of his second letter that we have to possess the privileges God offers to us freely. To have knowledge and power to do so does not come from within us, but from God ! We do not have the resources to be truly Godly. But God does allow us to "participate in the divine nature" in order to keep us from sin and to help us to live for Him. When we have been saved, God by His Holy Spirit empowers us with His own moral goodness. God gives us numerous promises in His word. I will mention only four in this devotion. They are...

A promise of pardon that converts, Acts 3:19
A promise of purity that calms, Acts 15:8-9
A promise of peace that abides with us, Philippians 4:7
A promise of power that conquers, Acts 1:8

A promise is a promise, especially when made by God!

AUGUST 26
SCRIPTURE: COLOSSIANS 3:1 (TEV)

"You have been raised to life with Christ, so set your hearts on the things that are in heaven, where Christ sits on His throne at the right side of God."

The hymn writer of the song "Turn Your Eyes Upon Jesus" tells us how to set our hearts on Jesus, who provides us with salvation and eternal love and faithfulness.

Listen to these words:
"Turn Your Eyes Upon Jesus,
Look full in His wonderful face.
And the things of earth will grow strangely dim,
In the light of His glory and grace!"

What a remarkable truth!

Modern technology has provided us with an instrument that will show us where we are located at any time. It is called a global positioning system (GPS). It even can direct one back to their home while travelling. It simply shows on the screen these words: "Go home." Wouldn't it be profitable if we could push a button and God would show us the way to our heavenly home? However, believers know that God has provided us with the way to that heavenly home through His plan of salvation by accepting Jesus Christ as our Savior. These suggestions of actions will move you in that direction: open your day with prayer requesting guidance; bring your daily activities to Him; consider your choices with God's purposes in mind; act on your choices; and thank God at the end of the day! It is God's day and God's way!

AUGUST 27
SCRIPTURE: ROMANS 12:2 (THE MESSAGE)

"Don't become so well-adjusted to your culture that you fit into it without even thinking. Instead, fix your attention on God. You'll be changed from the inside out."

God has given us the way to walk in our journey of life. In fact, the way has been stated in the Bible as the "straight and narrow." If this way works for you, then "you will be changed from the inside out." This balance of "inside out" is like the balancing act of a tightrope walker. When you are balanced within, it is demonstrated outside by your actions, words, and deeds. God knows, because He created us, that we cannot constantly walk the straight and narrow. We know from our own life experiences that the path we travel is winding, unlevel, laced with side roads, covered with potholes, includes detours, dips through the valleys, and climbs over the hills. Each of our journeys replicates the challenges of the ages.

God is involved and concerned about how we are able to live with these challenges of sin, grace, faith, calling, service, death and a host of life experiences. We know that God desires what is best for each of us. It has been written, "God works on us, reached out to us, and makes Himself known to us." In His relationships with us, He provides the trinity to assist us to gain the balance inside of those who have accepted His son as our personal Savior! As with the tightrope walker, God allows us in our journey to teeter from side to side while still loving us with His faithfulness.

AUGUST 28
SCRIPTURE: JOHN 11:26 (TEV)

"Jesus said to Martha, 'Whoever lives and believes in me will never die. Do you believe this?'"

Every one of us needs to ponder (to consider carefully and thoroughly) this same question that Jesus asked Martha: "Do you believe this?" This story should add meaning to Jesus' question to us. From a novel by William Thackery, a Mr. Newman is introduced to us. He was a kind-hearted soldier and an old-fashioned gentleman who lost his fortune and died in an alms house. Upon his deathbed, He pulled his hands from under the covers and kept time with the ringing of a bell in a nearby chapel. With the last ring, Mr. Newman lifted his head from his pillow and feebly said, "Adsum." This word means "present" in Latin. After stating the word, Mr. Newman immediately died. It was later learned that in his school days, he had used the word "adsum" to answer the roll. Even in his near death state, he hears the master calling his name. You see, Mr. Newman was present with God. All believers one day will be present with the Lord.

AUGUST 29
SCRIPTURE: HEBREWS 1:1–4 (TEV)

"In the past, God spoke to our ancestors many times and in many ways through the Prophets, but in these last days, He has spoken to us through His son. He is the one through whom God created the universe, the one whom God has chosen to possess all things at the end. He reflects the brightness of God's glory and is the exact likeness of God's own being, sustaining the universe with His powerful word. After achieving forgiveness for the sins of mankind, He sat down in heaven at the right side of God, the Supreme Power."

This scripture is a powerful and true statement that accurately describes Jesus Christ. It gives us justification as to why He is called Lord! Perhaps we forget when we hear of Jesus in the Bible, we also see the Father God. Read this one-sentence prayer and see if it has meaning for you. I pray this prayer daily.

"Lord, come into my heart, take control of my life, and make me the person that you created me to be. Amen." This prayer is not a verse of scripture, but it has deep meaning and value for every Christian. To say that Jesus is special is a gross understatement of His majesty and power. He is the exact likeness of Almighty God.

AUGUST 30
SCRIPTURE: LAMENTATIONS 3:22-24 (TEV)

"The Lord's unfailing love and mercy still continue, fresh as the morning, as sure as the sunrise. The Lord is all I have, and so in Him, I put my hope."

This statement is attributed to Virginia Woolf: "So that you may become children of the light...arrange what even pieces come your way." How do we handle those pieces of light in our lives? It appears from the above scripture that God's love is the major component of our action and deeds because of its continuing availability to those who seek such. The Lord's plan for us is like the fisherman's plan of catch and release. When successful, this plan includes: catch a fish, do not harm it, and gently let it go! In your spiritual life, catch the spirit of the Lord, gently internalize that spirit, and release it to those whom God brings your way.

AUGUST 31
SCRIPTURE: ISAIAH 55:8-9 (NRSV)

"For my thoughts are not your thoughts, nor are your ways my ways, says the Lord. For as the heavens are higher than the earth, so are my ways higher than your ways and my thoughts than your thoughts."

This scripture indicates to us that God Almighty should be consulted and involved in our plans, especially those plans concerning our spiritual life. In deciding and implementing our plan requires realistic goals, choices, not chance determines our best plans. Our journey in life is filled with planning. Most are successful, some require changes, and others do not develop at all. Think about this: our spiritual plans do not come to us automatically. These plans require our full participation and involvement with the Lord because His ways and thoughts are higher than ours. Listen to this plan of the British government during WWII. That government formed a commission to create sign posters to encourage the people to stay the course.

The first poster in September 1939:

> Your courage
> Your cheerfulness
> Your resolution
> Will bring
> Us victory

Shortly thereafter, the second poster was distributed:

> Freedom is
> In peril
> Defend it
> With all
> Your might

These two posters appeared all over the British countryside. The third poster was never distributed. Some 2.5 million copies were found sixty years later. The message was this: Keep calm and carry on! England did just that without encouragement of posters. Today, we need to trust God, turn your plan over to God, and keep calm and carry on! God loves us!!

SEPTEMBER 1
SCRIPTURE: EXODUS 19:5–6 (TEV)

"Now, if you will obey me and keep my covenant, you will be my own people. The whole earth is mine, but you will be my own people, a people dedicated to me alone, and you will serve me as Priests."

We believe in ONE God! Where does this belief come from? If we believe in the Holy Bible, the above scripture presents to us the Lord our God speaking to Moses and telling him, "You will be my own people!" From the beginning of human history, every culture, and every civilization, humankind has pondered the existence of God or of gods. Some created their own gods—metal sculptures and carvings of wood or stone. They created rituals and worship to please their gods. However, the Hebrew people believed in the existence of only one eternal, Almighty God! Beside Him, there were no other gods. Belief in our God usually brings about two questions: What is God like? What does God want? Jesus Himself tells us in numerous scriptures in the New Testament that God is the Father in Heaven. In John 14:11, Jesus tells the disciples, "Believe me when I say that I am in the Father and the Father is in me. If not, believe because of the things I do." What does God want? God wants us to reflect the light of His son to all the world so that we may gain salvation.

SEPTEMBER 2
SCRIPTURE: ECCLESIASTES 3:1 (NRSV)

"For everything there is a season, and a time for every matter under Heaven."

The first eight verses of the above scripture list some of humankind's actions displayed during good and bad behaviors. There is so much destructive behavior in our society today. I thought it would be positive just to explore the happy happenings list by the author of Ecclesiastes in the eight verses aforementioned. There is a time for: birth, planting, healing, building, dancing, making love, kissing, finding, saving, mending, talking, loving, and finding peace. All of these actions are a part of humankind's life realities that offer a coming together for healing and reconciliation.

The Book of James 1:19-20 presents three simple instructions for coming together: be quick to listen, be slow to speak, be slow to anger. Note: God gave us two ears to listen and one mouth to talk. God may have intended for us to listen twice as much as for us to talk. Think about that!

SEPTEMBER 3
SCRIPTURE: REVELATION 21:3 (TEV)

"I heard a loud voice speaking from the throne; 'now God's home is with humankind! He will live with them, and they shall be His people. God Himself will be with them, and He will be their God.'"

Closely linked to questions about eternity and eternal life are questions about the reality of heaven. Jesus left heaven to come to earth, so His words (especially in Revelation) about heaven should be considered as authentic and factual. Revelation is presented with symbolic words because it is describing the heavenly, celestial place of God and our future home. However, John also gives us vivid explanations in plain language; i.e., "God will wipe away all tears from their eyes. There will be no more death, no more grief, or crying or pain. The old things have disappeared." It is not possible to receive any more assuring words. Praise God!

SEPTEMBER 4
SCRIPTURE: PSALMS 73:25-27 (TEV)

"What else do I have in heaven but you? Since I have you, what else could I want on earth? My mind and my body may grow weak, but God is my strength; He is all I ever need."

Giving thanks to God forms in our hearts an attitude toward life that fosters enjoyment of what we already have and an attitude that opens the door for greater things to come. It sometimes seems that being thankful to God and others is seldom practiced by many. Do we still have reason to thank the Lord? Or to share our expressions of thanks with others? Is thanking God verbally too Old Testament? Too fundamental? Do we feel out of place using this expression?

The verbal expressions of thanks should be used often. These expressions help the person proclaiming it; it helps the person receiving the thanks; and it pleases God.

SEPTEMBER 5
SCRIPTURE: PSALMS 30: 11–12 (TEV)

"You have changed my sadness into a joyful dance; you have taken away my sorrow and surrounded me with joy. So I will not be silent; I will sing praises to you. Lord, you are my God; I will give you thanks forever."

Obviously, conversion has occurred in this psalmist's life and he is expressing those qualities of new life, which include for him joyful dance, song, praise, joy, and thankfulness. All seems to be well with him. But look at this verse closer. Look at his response: "I will not be silent."

Unlike many of us, the psalmist wants to voice his praise because God has changed his life. He wants to sing about it! This same theme of response is found throughout the Book of Psalms. But we can find an endless list of reasons why we remain silent, like, "I can't communicate well; I don't like to discuss religion; or this subject is too personal."

It is frightening to consider that our conversion story may be the only such "song of praise" that someone may hear. As verbally clumsy as we may be, God can allow the hearer to be influenced. Make an effort to be bolder in your witness. After all, it is God who moves the person to decision, but God could use your words and experiences.

Do as the psalmist; be determined not to be silent. You never know how God can use your story to win someone else.

SEPTEMBER 6
SCRIPTURE: 2 CORINTHIANS 8:7 (TEV)

"You are so rich in all you have: in faith, speech, and knowledge, in your eagerness to help and in your love for us. And so we want you to be generous also in this service of love."

Paul was writing to the Church in Corinth to appeal to this church for a generous offering to help the needy Christians in Judea. Look back above at the list of blessings that the people gave of their gifts, given to them by God. Paul said, "It was more than we could have hoped for." Here's His reasoning and He states it to them: "First they gave themselves to the Lord; then by God's will, they gave themselves to us as well." Now here's the amazing things of Paul's list about the riches given by the church people: the list does not even mention financial gifts. Is that not strange? Paul then makes this most astounding statement in verse 12 of this chapter: "If you are eager to give, God will accept your gift on the basis of what you have to give, not on what you don't have." God will present opportunities for you to give, "if you are eager to give."

SEPTEMBER 7
SCRIPTURE: EXODUS 3:7–8 (TEV)

"Then the Lord said, 'I have seen how cruelly my people are being treated in Egypt; I have heard them cry out to be rescued from their slave drivers. I know all about their sufferings, and so I have come down to rescue them from the Egyptians.'"

From this scripture and others, we learn that it is the desire for the Trinity to be for his people and to be with his people. For believers, we know that to be true, even though we have not seen God, Jesus, or the Holy Spirit. Let me suggest from scripture just one theme for each (God, Jesus, and Holy Spirit) of their being for us and for their being in us. First, we see in the scripture that God tells Moses, "I have come down to rescue them (His people) from the Egyptians." Second, we know of Jesus actual, physical birth on earth. Third, we know that the Holy Spirit was sent to believers: in fact to abide in us.

God's gifts are not on behalf of any particular people (except for the believers) who are honorable, worthy, or impressive. His gifts are to add well-being to His people and to enhance their lives. We should respond with Christ-like living. He still is for us and with us even today.

SEPTEMBER 8
SCRIPTURE: MATTHEW 17:1 & 5 (TEV)

"Six days later Jesus took with Him Peter and the brothers, James and John, and led them up a high mountain where they were alone. While He was talking, a shining cloud came over them, and a voice from the cloud said, 'This is my own dear son with whom I was pleased—Listen to Him!'"

Jesus may have taken the three disciples up on the mountain with the plan to worship God. What a worship service for Jesus and those present! And what wonder must have occurred! By the time Jesus reached the mountaintop, He was ready for worship! "Worship might best be defined as the act of magnifying God. Our goal, then, is simply to stand before God with a prepared and willing heart and let God do His work" (Max Lucado). Plan to worship asking God for an experience of worship with you!

SEPTEMBER 9
SCRIPTURE: MATTHEW 25:45–46 (TEV)

"I tell you, whenever you refused to help one of these least important ones, you refused to help me. These, then, will be sent off to eternal punishment, but the righteous will go to eternal life."

As we grow in our own spirituality, we have the opportunity to look back and see how far we have come to be a gift of service to others. It is not necessary that we all stand in the same place. As believers, enjoying relationships of love, we become help-mates in our journey of life. You see, God uses people in relationships with each other to enhance our own lives. Of all the ways the Lord reaches for us, none is more fundamental than life in togetherness. Faithful believers have a responsibility of not cutting off a relationship with anyone. Relationships are the fundamental truth at the heart of the doctrine of the Holy Trinity, which can be seen in the Father, the Son, and the Holy Spirit. By their grace, we have been promised the way to home in heaven. So look around for a brother in need and ask how best to serve him. God will be blessed, and so will you.

SEPTEMBER 10
SCRIPTURE: EPHESIANS 5:1
AND 1 PETER 2:9 (NRSV)

"Be imitators of God, as beloved children, and live in love, as Christ loves us."
"That you may proclaim the praises of Him who called you out of darkness into His marvelous light."

These two scriptures seem to flow together even though they are from different writers in the New Testament. All human beings are real and we can authenticate such in many ways; by height, weight, coloring, heartrate. Sometimes, we refer to persons as being real in their ability to communicate in ways that seem to reflect real truth, sensitivity, and spirituality. Their ability to understand with care and compassion is present in their acts, words, and behavior. These are people whom we refer to as being real. They are spiritually real, possessing Christ-like qualities. In order to become imitators of the Lord, we must be born again and accept Jesus as our personal Savior. Then, we become the real people that God created us to be.

SEPTEMBER 11
SCRIPTURE: ISAIAH 30:21 (TEV)

"If you wander off the road to the right or the left, you will hear His voice behind you saying, 'Here is the road. Follow it!'"

Below are the opening words spoken by "Christian" as He begins His "Pilgrim's Progress" journey. He sees a man and states, "I saw him open the book and read out of it, and as he read, he wept and trembled. Unable to contain himself any longer, he broke out with a sorrowful cry, saying, "What shall I do?" Many of us have found ourselves at some point in our life's journey "walking through the wilderness of this world," asking, "what shall I do?" Have you heard the expression "travelling down life's highway?" Much of literature and poetry refers to life as a journey that we travel from birth to death, experiencing the hills, the flatlands, and the valleys that we must travel through. God wants movement toward Him and toward the upward mobility of others. We need to be like infants learning to walk; they reach out and move toward someone, usually their parents. God also wants this same movement toward Him, our heavenly Father.

SEPTEMBER 12
SCRIPTURE: PSALM 130:5-6 (NRSV)

"I wait for the Lord, my soul waits and in His word I hope; my soul waits for the Lord more than those who watch for the morning, more than those who watch for the morning."

Waiting is one of the most difficult actions required of humankind. The psalmist also suffered from this same problem. Spiritually speaking, waiting on the Lord, can create a kind of intimacy that we seldom consider. Just attending church service does not satisfy God or us. The hardest part of waiting on the Lord is listening and then acting. If you listen and wait, the Lord has something to say to you. You will never hear His words until you listen! As Christians, we are called to have compassion for others. We may say, "What impact can I make, just little me?" However, we must remember God will always use and multiply what we have, if we step out in faith. No one can do everything, but everyone can do something!!

SEPTEMBER 13
SCRIPTURE: JAMES 5:16 (TEV)

"So then, confess your sins to one another and pray for one another, so that you will be healed. The prayer of a good person has a powerful effect."

Young, able-bodied man…
Post-surgery diagnosis, cancer…
Distraught young man…
Brokenhearted spouse and children…
Frightened parents, family, and friends.

Believing wife, requesting prayer…
Questioning young man, but willing to try…
Loving elders, gathered to pray…
Believers offering intercessory prayers…
Laying on of hands and tears of expectation.

Presence of God, noted by those gathered…
Deep sense of God's power working…
Sincerity of prayers and feeling generated…
Much hugging and crying experienced…
Knowledge of God's mystical power at work.

Next doctor's visit, no cancer…
Physician unable to explain…
Elated young man, thankful wife…
Relieved family, children, and friends…
Resurgence of faith among the believers.

I talked with this young man last week, now almost four years since that final report. He has regularly scheduled physical exams with still no sign of cancer. Both he and I agreed that what happened in that meeting was the most powerful happening that we had ever experienced.

Young, able bodied man…
Present diagnosis, cancer free…
Spirit-filled young man…
Thankful family, children, and friends…
Believers witnessed a miracle, THE POWER OF GOD!

SEPTEMBER 14
SCRIPTURE: I JOHN 1:7 (NRSV)

"If we walk in the light as Jesus Himself is in the light, we have fellowship with one another, and the blood of Jesus His son cleanses us from all sin."

The fact that Jesus walked through the pages of the New Testament was a two-sided action! He walked all over the general country known as Palestine. The events of His spiritual journeys have given us great insight into the character of God Almighty. Walking somehow seemed to fit into His plan of evangelizing. He was right there among the people. He could reach out and touch them, both physically and spiritually. These were the people He loved and the places He travelled. In Jesus' encounters as He walked the earth, no one ever met Him face to face and remained the same; and we can still say that is true today with confidence and assurance.

SEPTEMBER 15
SCRIPTURE: PSALM 107: 19–20 (NRSV)

"Then they cried to the Lord in their trouble, and He saved them from their distress; He sent out His word and healed them, and delivered them from destruction."

The psalmist in this chapter is speaking of people in distress. The words are a clear and true statement that was reflected in biblical times and are certainly a sad truth in today's society. Some situations of distress are brought about by our own words or actions; some by words or actions that are conditions beyond our control. Distress is mind-boggling and hazardous to our general, physical, and spiritual health. The statements from the psalmist name four groups of distress. They are wanderers, prisoners, sick, and storm-tossed. Thankfulness was constantly on the lips of those whom God saved. This Psalm states four actions on the part of distressed persons: they praise God's works, they recount the blessings of righteous living, they thank God for deliverance, and they praise God for His wonderful words. This statement comes from the last verse of this chapter: "Let those who are wise, give heed to these things, and consider the steadfast love of God."

SEPTEMBER 16
SCRIPTURE: I PETER 5:7–10 (NRSV)

"Like a roaring lion your adversary, the devil, prowls around, looking for someone to devour. Resist him, steadfast in your faith, for you know that your brothers and sisters in all the world are undergoing the same kinds of suffering."

In Peter's first letter to the scattered Christians whom he refers to as God's chosen and destined people. Peter's purpose was to encourage them to keep their faith. He was reminding them of the good news of Jesus Christ whose death, resurrection, and promised second coming should give them hope. In light of these facts, the people should accept and endure suffering. This is also great advice for the people of our time. It would appear that Peter is saying that the suffering people are sharing their despair with others in all the world. Peter is reminding us to remember that God recognizes that others matter to him, as we do, and he will remain faithful to us in our time of distress and sorrow.

SEPTEMBER 17
SCRIPTURE: PSALM 66:20 (NRSV)

"Blessed be to God because He has not rejected my prayer or removed His steadfast love from me."

For most English-speaking people, the acronym ASAP means "as soon as possible." This acronym is used very often, but sometimes Christians use it for this meaning: "Always say a prayer." You may be facing a problem that leaves you feeling helpless; i.e., loss of job, difficult family situation, health struggles or death of a loved one or close friend. Remember, ASAP! Often we do not; why? Why does God not answer our prayer request? You think all these requests are in God's will; you plead, you wait, then doubt creeps into your mind or faith. Then you stop asking God for a while. We really don't think much about prayers. We know exactly what prayer does for us. Prayer centers us; strengthens us; gives us peace, courage, wisdom, and insight; and makes us kinder. What then does prayer do for God? Prayer is not a transaction with God where He answers if we pray with more faith, pray harder, or pray more often. We know that God wants what is best for us as His children. Basically, prayer is our deepest act of trust in God. In prayer, we move to the depths of God's love from the depths of our love. Help us, God, as we pray to you with believing hearts!

SEPTEMBER 18
SCRIPTURE: GENESIS 33:1–3 & 10 (TEV)

"Jacob went ahead of them and bowed down to the ground seven times as he approached Esau. Esau had four hundred men with him." Verse 10 "Jacob said, 'to see your face is for me like seeing the face of God now that you have been so friendly to me.'"

Why do you suppose Jacob made this statement (above)? Then Jacob gives us a clue: "Now that you have been so friendly to me." There is power in receiving. Remember, in earlier actions, Jacob had taken advantage of their ailing father and had gotten his father, in effect, to change his will to favor Jacob over his older brother, Esau. After living about twenty years with such guilt, fear, alienation, and separation, Jacob was about to come face to face with his older brother. He may have even thought that Esau and his four hundred men were going to attack.

Here is the beauty of this story! Esau ran to meet Jacob to offer him acts of love. He took Jacob in his arms, held him to his chest, hugged him, and kissed him on the neck…and they cried together. When Esau let go of Jacob and Jacob could finally speak, he said to Esau, "I saw your face and it looked like God!" Jacob was so surprised at the acts of love demonstrated to him by Esau. Jacob received an unexpected hug, an unbelievable reception, unearned forgiveness, undeserved love, and heartfelt acceptance. Esau's actions may show us ways to make amends with others whom we have wronged.

SEPTEMBER 19
SCRIPTURE: JOB 2:13 (NRSV)

"They sat with him on the ground seven days and seven nights, and no one spoke a word to Job, for they said that his suffering was very great."

This scripture depicts Job's three friends who came to help Job through his tremendous loss of his family and all his belongings. Their togetherness may be the longest time for just sitting with a hurting friend. What does "sitting a spell" mean to you? In my younger days, I remember older family members just saying, "Well, I think I'll go over to Robert's house and sit a spell!" Not visit a while, not take a pie over, not going over and discussing a specific subject.

I even wondered if "sitting for a spell" even involved any conversation. I have realized as I have grown older that activity during the sitting spell did not really matter. What really mattered was that someone did not have to sit alone. Today, we seldom visit with one another. And yet one of the most personal and gracious gifts we can give to anyone is our time. We cannot make, manufacture, or buy more time. I've used the phrase "to sit a spell" to make a point. But the real point is "being present" for another who is in need or hurting. Sometimes you feel that you have to be patient and listen. A great lesson learned is that you don't have to have the answers . Your presence is what is needed.

SEPTEMBER 20
SCRIPTURE: MATTHEW 5:16 (TEV)

"in the same way your light must shine before people, so that they will see the good things you do and praise your Father in Heaven."

Jesus has shown us the example to use as we "shine before people." That example is His very life. To a small band of believers, He passed the torch and generation after generation of Christians have attempted to carry forth those examples. The Olympic torch bearer, before each of the international festivals, runs with an ever-increasing pace, carrying the torch that then bursts into a large, continuously glowing flame. That flame raises the spirits of the participants and spectators to a high level of excitement.

In our Christian life, the spiritual torch has been passed to us from the Source to be shared with those involved in our journey. He places a large responsibility on us. He moved on and we are to step in. Just as His manner of life and His speech was the light that showed the way out of darkness, so must we continue that work.

SEPTEMBER 21
SCRIPTURE: JAMES 3:8–10 (NRSV)

"No one can tame the tongue, a restless evil full of deadly poison. With it we bless the Lord and Father, and with it we curse those who are made in the likeness of God. From the same mouth comes blessing and cursing. This ought not to be so."

Have you ever said, "I had to bite my tongue to keep from saying something?" Why? Why would we have to take such drastic action against our tongue to keep from expressing ourselves? What is it about the tongue that requires such a tight bridle for control. King David even said, "I will guard against my ways that I may not sin with my tongue." Remember, one of the fruits of the spirit is self-control. Self-control could well be the key to control of our tongue.

Generally, when we consider our self-control, we think in terms of our actions that control our behavior. God knew what He was doing when He made our tongues attached at one end; otherwise, we would be in constant trouble: "tongues loose at both ends."

SEPTEMBER 22
SCRIPTURE: 1 TIMOTHY 3:16–17 (NRSV)

"All scripture is inspired by God and is useful for teaching, for reproof, for correction, and for training in righteousness, so that everyone who belongs to God may be proficient, equipped for every good work."

One of the most important facts about the scripture is that it reveals to us who God is like and how we can be reconciled to Him through His son, Jesus Christ. Perhaps the safest course in establishing your spiritual beliefs is to let the Bible speak for itself. God does not impose His word upon us. He loves us enough to give us free will to experience and accept His way, which is reported in the scriptures of the Holy Bible. We are not left to chance on which to rest our lives and eternity. The Bible reports; you decide!

SEPTEMBER 23
SCRIPTURE: 1 JOHN 4:11 (NRSV)

"If God so loved us, we ought also to love one another."

A commercial on TV pointed out that the word LIFE has two letters between the L and E; it forms the word IF. The word IF is a conjunction connecting words and phrases that carry a condition. When I consider the word LIFE with IF between the L and the letter E, these thoughts come to mind: The letter L represents the light (Jesus) and the letter E represents evil (the devil). The IF then represents us, who live our lives between good and the evil. Can you think of anything in life as full as the "IFS"? It really is another way of saying life is full of choices. There is a state of indecision associated with the word IF. We can make bold, brave statements of intentions that lose boldness when the statement is punctuated with the word IF. IF always leaves us a way out. "I'm going to church on Sunday IF I don't go to New Orleans."

SEPTEMBER 24
SCRIPTURE: MARK 11:20–21 (NRSV)

"As they passed by, they saw the fig tree withered away to its roots…. Peter said to Jesus, 'Rabbi, look! The fig tree that you cursed has withered.'"

The cursing of the fig tree was an "acted out" parable by Jesus for the benefit of the disciples and for us. The fig tree showed promise of fruit, but it produced none. Jesus was showing His anger at the religious life without substance. If you claim to have faith without putting it to work in your life, you will be like the barren fig tree. The fig tree looked promising but offered no fruit—much like Israel, which had the appearance only, but was spiritually barren. Be sure that your faith does not become barren in your life's journey!

SEPTEMBER 25
SCRIPTURE: PHILIPPIANS 3:13–14 (TEV)

"The one thing I do, is to forget what is behind me and do my best to reach what is ahead. So I run straight toward the goal in order to win the prize, which is God's call through Christ Jesus to the life above."

Paul writes of the joy and peace that God gives to those who live in union with Christ. It would appear that he could well be writing this letter to us! How many times do you say to yourself or others, "I have to do such and such." "I have to." That expression in itself puts extra pressure on us. "I have to!" My suggestion to you is simply this: substitute that expression with the phrase "I need to!" You'll be surprised at how much less stress you put on yourself. Try it!

SEPTEMBER 26
SCRIPTURE: LUKE 6:12 & 13 (NRSV)

"Jesus went out to the mountain to pray and He spent the night in prayer to God. And when day came, He called His disciples and chose twelve of them, whom He named Apostles."

Jesus' choice of His followers was not by happenstance! While Jesus loved the many, in this case He focused on the few. And thank God, He still focuses on the few, including you and me. Let me share three defining practices about prayer: 1) selection; it is acceptable for you to pray that God will help you to select who and what to pray for; 2) intercessory prayer, which is to determine how you need to pray for the person you chose; 3) covenant prayer, where you and another person mutually agree to pray regularly for each other. In Matthew 18:19, Jesus says, "I tell you that if two of you on earth agree about anything you ask for, it will be done for you by my Father in Heaven." If you are serious about your prayers, use the three techniques listed above.

SEPTEMBER 27
SCRIPTURE: JUDGES 21:25 (NRSV)

"In those days there was no King in Israel; all the people did what was right in their own eyes."

We as Christians need to return to the teachings of God's Holy Word as presented to us in the Bible. Our society today suffers from new records of dishonesty, disrespect, sexual promiscuity, violence, suicide, and other destructive behaviors that indicate a loss of moral values and beliefs. Truth has been eroded. Many in our age do not believe that anything can be definitely defined as right or wrong unless they experience it. Humankind has not changed much over the centuries. Have we? We still determine what is "right in our own eyes." We need to return to a sure foundation that presents values without exceptions. "If you don't believe in something, you will believe in anything."

SEPTEMBER 28
SCRIPTURE: I CORINTHIANS 13:1 (TEV)

"I may be able to speak the language of men and even of angels, but if I have no love, my speech is no more than a noisy gong or a clanging bell."

Paul in the above scripture is part of the chapter we know as the "Love Chapter." If God is love, then the language of love must be the desired language that God means and demonstrates for us to use when we communicate with Him and others. God demonstrates in numerous statements of scripture that He wants to be in a relationship of love with His precious humankind. "God is love, and those who abide in love abide in God, and God abides in them." A few years ago, an interesting song stated, "What the world needs now is love, sweet love. That's the only thing that we need plenty of." In the Book of Micah, he simply states, "what God requires of us is this: to do what is just, to show constant love, and to live in humble fellowship with our God." What then should be our language in our relationships with others who come our way in life? Love, love, love!

SEPTEMBER 29
SCRIPTURE: MALACHI 3:10 (NRSV)

"This put me to the test, says the Lord of Hosts; see if I will not open the windows of heaven for you and pour down for you an overflowing blessing."

God's promise of "overflowing blessings" is not limited to just monetary blessing! Note in Luke 6:38, Jesus states, "Give, and it will be given to you. A good measure, pressed down, shaken together, running over, will be put into your lap; for the measure you give will be the measure you get back." Please notice when you forgive you will receive: "a good measure, pressed down, shaken together, running over, and poured into your lap." Apparently, the overflowing blessings that God promises to pour out are in the spiritual realm. When the Lord throws open the "windows of heaven," the sunlight of His love streams forth. That sunlight is a reflection of God's blessings of His love, mercy, and grace; these make up a good foundation for our future. God wants us rich in our acts, words, deeds, and relationship with Him and with others.

SEPTEMBER 30
SCRIPTURE: PSALM 121:2–3 AND 7–8 (TEV)

"My help will come from the Lord, who made heaven and earth. He will not let you fall; your protector is always awake. The Lord will protect you from all danger; He will keep you safe. He will protect you as you come and go now and forever."

The above scripture says to us that God has plans for our entire lives. He even knew us before our birth. Your life has profound meaning for Him and for you. First Timothy 4:12 offers Timothy advice from Paul as to how Timothy should conduct himself: "Be an example for believers in your speech, your conduct, your love, faith, and purity." God has a purpose for your life, and His motive for creating you was His amazing love. God is love!

OCTOBER 1
SCRIPTURE: EZEKIEL 22:30 (NRSV)

"So I sought for a man among them who would make a wall, and stand in the gap before me on behalf of the land, that I should not destroy it; but I found no one."

Physical walls were built around most of the towns in biblical times for the protection of the people. Spiritual walls were spoken that groups of faithful people united in their efforts to resist evil and to worship the Lord . Now, both the physical and spiritual walls have been breached, which allows entrance into the protected area. The Lord was using an example of the gap left by the breach in a wall, only He was speaking of a spiritual wall. When these gaps occurred, immediate attention was required for continued protection from enemies of the community. The Lord was saying that Israel's wall of His chosen people was being breached by foreign enemies. He wanted a person to step forward to initiate a plan to change the mind-set of the people to move back into a healing and following of His way. He could not find one person to fill the gap. The spiritual walls of our time desperately needed many persons to stand in the spiritual gap! Some of the same type conditions of our day are akin to those of Ezekiel's time. In God's wall, a gap is very repairable. We should all be caretakers of His wall and to stand in the gaps.

OCTOBER 2
SCRIPTURE: I TIMOTHY 1:13–14 (TEV)

"God was merciful to me because I did not yet have faith and so did not know what I was doing. And our Lord poured out His abundant grace on me and gave me the faith and love which are ours in union with Christ Jesus."

These two verses spoken by Paul to Timothy sum up conversion in a concise manner. To review the verses after your spiritual experience only intensifies your desire to thank and praise God. It is an amazing thing to learn that God was merciful to me even when I did not have faith. This is a fact that we cannot fully appreciate until we accept Jesus and come to know Him. He loves us all the while, even when we don't know what we are doing, in a spiritual sense. Then after conversion, because we are in union with Christ, God pours out His abundant grace and gives us faith and love.

If we knew before conversion what we now know, after conversion, we would have sought it at all cost. But now we know that Jesus paid our cost and that the faith and love are freely given to us without condition through God's grace.

In God's scheme of salvation for His people, are not these two verses descriptive of our most precious gift? And this is available for each of us!

OCTOBER 3
SCRIPTURE: ROMANS 12:9–13 (NRSV)

"Let love be genuine; hate what is evil, hold fast to what is good. Love one another with mutual affection; outdo one another in showing honor. Do not lag in zeal, be ardent in spirit, serve the Lord. Rejoice in hope, be patient in suffering, persevere in prayer, contribute to the needs of the saints; extend hospitality to strangers."

Law enforcement personnel are sometimes accused of profiling in the pursuit of suspected law violators. Profiling is the use of a set of characteristics to identify those likely to belong to certain groups. If you were to profile a Christian, what characteristics would you look for to provide a clear representation of same? A good place to start is your Bible, the Book of Romans, 12:9-21. The subheading for these verses is "marks of the true Christian." We all seem to profile, either consciously or unconsciously. We even profile Christians! These verses cover numerous activities of the believer. We may even say that there are just too many or too much to identify. We forget about the Lord's help that is free to us, if we have faith and believe. All who have contact with us are watching our behavior, our words and actions. Remember to show them a profile of a Christian.

OCTOBER 4
SCRIPTURE: ISAIAH 9:6 (NRSV)

"For a child has been born for us, a son given to us; authority rests upon His shoulders; and He is named wonderful counselor, mighty God, everlasting Father, Prince of Peace."

The above scripture is prophesy from Isaiah in the Old Testament, and we know that it was fleshed out in the New Testament in the person of Jesus Christ. Several years ago, there was much discussion among the believers and non-believers alike regarding this subject: "What's the big deal about Jesus?" It would seem that any Christian could answer that question by stating Jesus Christ is our Lord and Savior! What you see in life is based on where you stand. Suppose you are standing on the field of an athletic sport. Your sight is limited to movement of a smaller area. The higher you go up into the stands, the better your view becomes as you can see the entire playing field. That same movement of elevation should be the goal of believers as we travel our life's journey. God's word gives us the elevated position as well as a model to show us how we should live. We should be about proclaiming Jesus Christ alone as the way of salvation, the truth of God's word, and the life of discipleship. Stand tall!

OCTOBER 5
SCRIPTURE: PSALM 16:11
AND MATTHEW 28:20 (NRSV)

"In thy presence is fullness of joy; at the right hand there are pleasures for evermore." "I will be with you always, to the end of the age."

We do not really summon the Lord to our side. He is already there, as is the Holy Spirit. In both Testaments, the Lord is saying that His presence is available for us. We know that He is all-wise, ever-present, and all-powerful. Perhaps you have heard of Brother Lawrence. In 1649, he entered a religious community of men in Paris and became a lay Brother and was given the name Brother Lawrence. At the convent, he was assigned to work in the kitchen washing dishes, pots, and pans. He was known as the "Lord of pots and pans." He developed a habit of talking with God throughout the day. He called it practicing the presence of God. What was his secret? To always know that God is near. He is quoted as saying, "There is not in the world a kind of life more delightful than that of a continual conversation with God." Open your heart to the presence of God Almighty and talk to Him every day!

OCTOBER 6
SCRIPTURE: COLOSSIANS 3:12–13 (NRSV)

"As God's chosen ones, holy and beloved, clothe yourselves with compassion, kindness, humility, meekness, and patience. Bear with one another and, if anyone has a complaint against another, forgive each other; just as the Lord has forgiven you, so you also must forgive."

Notice from the above scripture these precious words, "Bear with one another!" The dictionary gives these two meanings of "to bear": "to hold up or support" and "to be patient with!" Paul is saying that forgiveness is an action as well as a verbal command. The Lord wants us to be not just sayers of forgiveness but also to be doers of forgiveness. Let us look straight into the words of the above scripture and resolve, with help from Jesus Christ, that we will live with compassion, forgiveness, love, and peace in our hearts and lives with meaningful words for the believers: "I forgive!"

OCTOBER 7
SCRIPTURE: ROMANS 5:1–2 (TEV)

"Now that we have been put right with God through faith, we have peace with God through our Lord Jesus Christ. He has brought us by faith into this experience of God's grace, in which we now live and so we boast of the hope we have of sharing God's glory."

Faith in God provides each of us who decide to follow Him with His peace, His presence, and a progression toward Him. We need to make ourselves available for God to use. Step out in faith today and allow the Lord to work and move in your life. You are never too old to be someone's hero. We each have had spiritual heroes who have been influential in our journey. So think of how profound your statement of faith could be if you shared it with someone. All God wants us to do is just to step out and share your experience with Jesus to others. You don't have to cause the other person to internalize your faith and cause their heart to change—that's God's job: All the Lord wants us to do is share our faith. Our faith story may be the only one that some person may hear! Never be too timid to tell anyone what the Lord has done for you!

OCTOBER 8
SCRIPTURE: PSALM 139:23–24 (TEV)

"Examine me, O God, and know my mind; test me, and discover my thoughts. Find out if there is any evil in me and guide me in the everlasting way."

We as God's people seem to have the tendency to make life so difficult for ourselves, our families, our friends, and many others with whom we have dealings. God's word offers so many guidelines for how we should live. Hardly a page in the Bible is without instructions that give us His word or that of His chosen spokesperson. The Lord wants us to travel in our lives in a path of upward mobility. From the time of conversion, the Lord wants us to move from the flat level of worldly affairs, actions, and thinking to ever-increasing movement upward. The Lord wants us to seek higher ground. Psalm 128:2 declares, "You shall be happy and it shall go well with you." "All is well" does not mean that life is perfect or easy. It simply means that by God's love and grace, we can come to feel His embrace during times of difficult troubles. Move toward the Lord!

OCTOBER 9
SCRIPTURE: PSALM 32:5 AND PSALM 30:12 (TEV)

"I confessed my sins to you; I did not conceal my wrongdoings. I decided to confess them to you, and you forgave all my sins." "So I will not be silent; I will sing praise to you. Lord, you are my God; I will give you thanks forever."

We too can find the joy and peace in our act of confession of sins to God, as did David. We can also be about telling others of the same joy and peace. If we as professing Christians, who have accepted Jesus as our Savior, remain silent about the joy of salvation, who is to share God's love to the world? We can show that love through our witness, our love, our actions, our giving, our sharing, and our caring.

Our imaginations are our only limited as to how we answer His call, and demonstrate God's love for humankind. We can have David's mind-set and declare, "So I will not be silent." Someone asked a hearing-impaired man, "Why do you go to church each Sunday when you cannot hear the music, the songs, or the sermon? He wrote His reply: "I come each week to let the people know which side I am on." He was saying, "So I will not be silent!" What about you?

OCTOBER 10
SCRIPTURE: MATTHEW 13:14–15 (TEV)

"This people will listen and listen, but not understand; they will look and look, but not see. Because their minds are dull, and they have stopped up their ears and have closed their eyes. Otherwise, their eyes would see, their ears would hear, their minds would understand and they would turn to me, says God, and I would heal them."

The people of the Old Testament, like in the New Testament, have great difficulty in seeing God's way that He desires of His people. We use our eyes in a physical manner by perceiving images and bringing them into consciousness, awareness, and meaning for appropriate action.

That we may see spiritually is not the physical act of seeing with our eyes. But rather is the act of seeing and understanding with our hearts, minds, and souls. This type of seeing comes as a gift of grace given by God when we are redeemed. Fanny J. Crosby had a tremendous knowledge of this grace in her hymn "Saved by Grace." The chorus is:

> "And I shall see Him face to face,
> And tell the story—saved by grace."

You see, Fanny J. Crosby was blind from the age of six weeks, but what ability to see spiritually!

OCTOBER 11
SCRIPTURE: JAMES 1:13–14 (NRSV)

"If a person is tempted by trials, he must not say, 'This temptation comes from God.' For God cannot be tempted by evil and He Himself tempts no one. But a person is tempted when he is drawn away and trapped by His own evil desires."

Temptation comes from evil desires inside of us, not from God. It follows this pattern: An evil thought enters our mind; the temptation becomes sin; we allow it to become an action; the sin-action grows more destructive. One of the more frequently used methods to explain our temptation is blaming others. We all use this mechanism. Everybody is doing it; it's the other person's fault; I can't help it; it was just a mistake; nobody is perfect; the devil made me do it; I was pressured into the action; I didn't know the act was wrong or improper. The believer handles the sin by accepting responsibility for the act; confesses the act to God; and seeks God's forgiveness. Then change your mind-set and live a Christ-like life. All of the actions listed above work! Many have used one or more in their daily relationship with God and others. Any and all lead a person in a downward direction. Excuses, excuses! We need to praise, honor, and give thanks to God. After all, humankind was God's "first fruits" of all He created. With that designation, we need to remember who we are in our worship of the Lord.

"Then they cried to the Lord in their trouble, and He saved them from their distress: He sent out His word and healed them."

Several years ago in a TV ad for a drug that was introduced to help lower cholesterol, a man whose problem was reduced by the drug was expressing his joy by telling others, regardless of their knowledge of him or his medical condition. The man drives up beside the car of a stranger, rolls down his window, and shouts to the other driver, "My cholesterol is down," then drives off. Again, on an elevator with a stranger, he announces with excitement, "My cholesterol is lower!" When he gets to his office, he sticks his head in an ongoing staff meeting and announces, "My cholesterol level has been greatly lowered!" This was, needless to say, a happy man! God made us to share good news to others and thanksgiving to Him. The first two verses of Psalm 107 state, "O give thanks to the Lord, for he is good; for his steadfast love endures forever. Let the redeemed of the Lord say so!" When we are redeemed from our distress, we are relieved from pressure, anxiety, and guilt. Let us give praise to the Lord!

OCTOBER 13
SCRIPTURE: JOSHUA 24:13–14 (NRSV)

"I gave you a land on which you had not labored, and towns that you had not built, and you lived in them; you eat the fruit of vineyards and olive yards that you did not plant. Now therefore revere the Lord, and serve Him in sincerity and in faithfulness."

In chapter 24 of Joshua, the Lord explains all of His efforts to take His people from captives to freedom. In his book *The Bible Makes Sense*, Walter Brueggeman makes this point: "The God of the Bible is the strangest thing about the Bible. There is no other like this God of ours." You see, our God is both with His people and for His people. Throughout the Old Testament, God was always making covenants with Israel to demonstrate His faithfulness and His love. In these actions, God was proving His character of being with and for His people, and God extended these same two characteristics to us through the New Testament with the life, death, and resurrection of Jesus Christ. Just the knowledge of the Lord's being with us and for us should be of great assurance to each of us.

OCTOBER 14
SCRIPTURE: ISAIAH 54:2 (TEV)

"Make the tent you live in larger; lengthen its ropes and strengthen the pegs!"

This verse is in reference to the return of God's people to their homeland after being unproductive in captivity. He promises to them that things will be greatly improved upon their return. Growth and expansion should be expected. These actions are suggested, enlarged, lengthened, and strengthened. Also, these words have significance: tents, ropes, and pegs.

Suppose we consider our tent as our church; the ropes as those demonstrated elements that would bind us together—i.e., faith, tolerance, peace, love, fellowship, etc.; and the pegs as you and me. If we move toward a planned expectation of greater things for our church, we could consider this as an enlarged tent, lengthened ropes, and strengthened pegs.

An enlarged tent could mean an expanded membership, which is something that really needs our prayers, planning, and active pursuit. It appears that God is saying through Isaiah that greater things could be possible with growth: "make the tents you live in larger."

If we consider the ropes as those elements that bind us together, then God is saying to us collectively and individually, "Lengthen your ropes." Are we doing this?

And last, if we are the pegs, are we really being strengthened in our Christian journey? Have you ever noticed in putting up a tent, the closer you place the peg to the tent, the easier it is for the tent to topple? Perhaps we are too close, too steeped in our own tradition and our own comfortable pew. This entire verse suggests growth, personal and corporate. Are we moving in that direction?

OCTOBER 15
SCRIPTURE: JOHN 1:35–37 (NRSV)

"The next day John the Baptist again was standing with two of his disciples, and as he watched Jesus walk by, he exclaimed, 'Look, here is the lamb of God!' The two disciples heard him say this, and they followed Jesus."

Did you ever wonder why these two men just seem to follow Jesus with no explained reason? What got them started down the road to follow Jesus? John the Baptist did announce Jesus' presence by stating, "Look, here is the lamb of God." Was that statement too much for them to comprehend? Perhaps what really got them started was community. Andrew looked at the other disciple; He then looked at Andrew and one said, "Let's go." And they started—that's community. Remember the first time you jumped off a high diving board as a kid? What got you started climbing up the ladder? Did you decide with solitary courage to climb up the ladder or did some other kid say, "I'll jump if you will!" If it's too high for one person, it's too high for two. But you needed the other kid to join you in your illogical decision. We need community in our faith decision and journey. Sometimes it is too big a leap to do the things of God alone. Some can make the leap alone—those who live by the principle that "eagles fly alone." But all of us aren't eagles. We learn to soar in the flock. That's community. Get involved with fellow believers and soar together. That's community!

OCTOBER 16
SCRIPTURE: ISAIAH 60:19 (TEV)

"No longer will the sun be your light by day or the moon be your light by night; I, the Lord, will be your eternal light. The light of my glory will shine on you."

Combing this scripture with John 1:5, we see that "the light" is Jesus; "the light shines in the darkness, and the darkness has never put it out!" When it comes to issues of our day, we tend to interpret scripture in light of our own worldview. A "Jesus position" is not always clearly spelled out. However, if we live by those words that Jesus did speak, our behavior will truly reflect His way. Those other questions that Jesus does not answer will pale in the light of His stated words, as well as the examples of His life. I saw this bumper sticker several years ago that stated: "Read the Bible, it will scare the hell out of you." The Gospel of Mark seems to bring out a basic word about Jesus: "Jesus came preaching the Gospel of God." And that preaching, teaching, and healing has revolutionized the world. Has it touched you yet?

OCTOBER 17
SCRIPTURE: 2 CORINTHIANS 8:12 (TEV)

"If you are eager to give, God will accept your gift on the basis of what you have to give, not on what you don't have."

From *Guidepost* magazine, I read a sentence that really made an impression on me. It said, "Generosity is a condition of the heart, not the wallet." A working definition of generosity is: "a noble-minded, magnanimous willingness to give or share unselfishly." Jesus' generosity is seen in most of His teachings and actions. Each of us has known of the feeling of generosity in our walk as we experience relationships with others. We know that it is Christ-like to be generous in our giving of time, love, forgiveness, and patience and a whole host of acts of the heart. From beginning to end, all of life is a continuous gift given to us by God. We really deserve nothing. He owes us nothing. Yet, He gives us everything for us to live a Christian life. Sharing these blessings completes the purpose of generosity.

OCTOBER 18
SCRIPTURE: 1 CORINTHIANS 13:13 (NRSV)

"And now faith, hope, and love abide, these three, and the greatest of these is love."

I recently read these statements from a *Guidepost* article that listed words that reflect love to others. This statement was: "I love you," "I forgive you," and "I am sorry." They work well with spouses, families, and anyone else who is important to you. Each of these statements requires strong initiative, honesty, and your own style of relating. In some situations either of the statements may even be difficult to say to the other person. When you say, "I love you," you are opening yourself up for hopeful reactions that you may or may not receive. There are few statements that possess such potential for you, especially if you receive a positive response. When you say to someone, "I forgive you," you are able to do that because God first forgave you! Sometimes you have to build up much courage to tell someone, "I forgive you." It shouldn't be that way, but it is. When you say, "I am sorry," it is difficult because it has to come from a place deep within you that is generally hidden by pride or maybe even revenge. Let us love one another, because love is from God.

OCTOBER 19
SCRIPTURE: I TIMOTHY 3:16 (TEV)

"No one can deny how great is the secret of our religion. He (Jesus) appeared in human form, was shown to be right by the spirit, and was seen by angels. He preached among the nations, was believed in throughout the world and was taken up to heaven."

Jesus is referred to in Colossians as the "key that opens all the hidden treasures of God." Through Jesus, God gave each of us the key at the time of our repentance and conversion. Take your key, shine it with care, polish it with love, for your family, with service for friends; with help for the lonely and disenfranchised, remove all rust with prayers for our country, and worship the Lord with praise and thanksgiving. God's purpose in Jesus is to redeem those who were under the law, so that we might receive adoptions as His children. Handle the key with care and love.

OCTOBER 20
SCRIPTURE: JOHN 11:14–15 (NRSV)

"Then Jesus told them plainly, 'Lazarus is dead.' For your sake, I am glad I was not there, so that you may believe. But let us go to Him."

This scripture about Lazarus being raised from his state of death was used by Jesus to demonstrate His power, even over death, and Lazarus was raised by Jesus in the presence of the disciples. In verse 39 of the chapter Jesus said, "take away the stone," which had been rolled to the entrance of the tomb where Lazarus was buried. His resurrection could not happen until he was unbound and the stone was moved! Then Jesus cried out, "Lazarus, come out!" He came out of the tomb and his feet and hands were bound with strips of cloth. Then Jesus said to the gathered people, "Unbind him and let him go!" What lesson does this story of Lazarus teach us today? Think of the stone. Think of it as a blockage to people's ability to believe in God's love. Maybe, we all have stones in our lives that we cannot break through. The stones have to be rolled away by our faith in God. Maybe we can be a part in bringing others to the Lord by helping them to see the stones and encouraging them to look to God for freedom from the bondages holding them captive.

OCTOBER 21
SCRIPTURE: ISAIAH 43:1 (TEV)

"Do not be afraid—I will save you. I have called you by name—you are mine."

Maybe, when we read these and other beautiful words from the Old Testament, we might feel that God was speaking of someone else. Words so wonderful that we want to believe it could also be true about us. Because God's word is the living word, all scripture should be meaningful to us, as it was to Old Testament people. The Bible has hope and application for us today! For you and me! None of us can live by the whole word, obeying every command. So, by what measure do we then decide which scripture will guide our lives, share out thoughts, and govern our actions?

One of the most basic fundamental Christian beliefs is that the life of Jesus Christ is the best revelation of God ever seen by the world. That being true, Jesus is our best look at God; then we need to learn as much as we can about Jesus. We learn about Him through the study of the Gospels. Then we need to allow the Holy Spirit to empower us to believe that His words should become the standard by which we live.

OCTOBER 22
SCRIPTURE: ACTS 2:42 (TEV)

"They spent their time in learning from the Apostles, taking part in the fellowship, and sharing in meals and the prayers."

Many of the Christian churches of our time still use this scripture as a model for worshiping the Lord in regular Sunday services.

1. The Apostles teaching is considered the preaching.
2. The sharing in the fellowship is the singing, liturgy, Apostle's Creed, Lord's Prayer, etc.
3. The sharing of meals is celebrating in the participation of Holy Communion.
4. The prayers are basically the same prayers today, both individually and corporately.

The movement of the Christian church and its activities has been amazing for two thousand years, plus! Glory to God!

OCTOBER 23
SCRIPTURE: MATTHEW 20:30–34 (TEV)

"Two blind men were sitting by the road heard that Jesus was passing by, so they began to shout, 'Son of David! Have mercy on us, sir!'…. Jesus stopped and called to them. 'What do you want me to do for you?' He asked them. 'We want you to give us our sight!' Jesus had pity on them and touched their eyes; at once they were able to see, and they followed Him."

Jesus had compassion on the two blind men and perhaps experienced what Matthew Kelly defined in his book, *Rediscover Jesus,* as a Holy moment. His definition of a Holy moment is this: "A moment when you are being the person God created you to be, and you are doing what you feel God is calling you to do in that moment!" We tend, even as Christians, to carefully use the word *holy*. Even thinking of self as being Holy is not often considered. However, in 1 Thessalonians 4:3, may reduce the pressure of our mind-set and our actions toward being Holy . That scripture simply states, "God's will is for you to be Holy." Holiness is possible for us (you and me) today. God creates for us opportunities to experience a Holy moment! I believe that I composed this simple prayer after being moved by something I had heard on the radio; this is it: "Lord, come into my heart, take control of my life, and make me the person that you created me to be." Amen! A Holy moment experienced!

OCTOBER 24
SCRIPTURE: PROVERBS 4:18 (TEV)

"The road the righteous travel is like the sunrise, getting brighter and brighter until daylight has come."

The concept of a road has always been fascinating to me because it implies a course or way. Also to be considered are directions, movements, straight lines, curves, smooth surfaces, bumps and potholes, upgrades and downgrades, shoulders, and ditches. It would seem that roads and these implications mirror times of change, mobility, or the lack of same in our lives.

Illustrations of roads are often used in both the Old and New Testaments—for example, the road to Emmaus or the road on which the good Samaritan performed his deed of kindness and assistance. I have heard the expression "hit the road" all my life by those intending to travel.

God wants us to hit the road, to be travelers for Him. He wants us to be involved in movement, upward mobility, meeting and greeting on the road of life. Those who travel the WAY know that life also has its potholes and bumps, narrow lanes, and sometimes detours, as have most roads. This proverb offers great hope as we travel life's roads because spiritually the way gets brighter and brighter. Just as God directs the rise of the sun in this world, He also directs the sunrise in our hearts.

OCTOBER 25
SCRIPTURE: MATTHEW 11:28–29 (NRSV)

"Come to me…and learn from me; for I am gentle and humble in heart, and you will find rest for your souls. For my yoke is easy, and my burden is light."

Jesus still issues to us today the invitation "come to me." There also seems to be implied in the invitation a desire for a positive response from the one who hears. Our motivation for a response today is that we know that Jesus has revealed God to us! Christ is telling us to come to Him, to believe in Him, and to trust in Him and Him only, to gain salvation. In stating "take my yoke," Jesus is telling us that His yoke is easy, with the gentleness of His nature and the humbleness of His heart. Go to Jesus.

OCTOBER 26
SCRIPTURE: JEREMIAH 6:16 (TEV)

"Thus says the Lord; stand at the crossroads, and look, and ask for the ancient paths, where the good way lies; and walk in it, and find rest for your souls. But they said, 'We will not walk in it.'"

In this scripture, God is warning the people of Israel of catastrophic events they would suffer as a result of their idolatry and sin. And as God's people often did, they refused to heed the predictions that Jeremiah gave them. And sure enough, disaster followed. God's advice, through the prophet, was to "seek the ancient paths where the good way lies." The spiritual meaning of the good path" is "a moral course of conduct or thought to take when considering or making decisions." Then, God says to "walk in it!" We all know that the all-time, number one source to find the "good way" is to go to your Bible. It would appear that the people of our time have the same attitude as the people of Israel did in the Old Testament. People still say, "We will not walk in it!" Our points of life appear to be growing dimmer at a rapid pace! What will be His judgment upon us in our time?

OCTOBER 27
SCRIPTURE: PSALM 103:2–5 (NRSV)

"Bless the Lord, O my soul, and do not forget all His benefits; who forgives all your iniquity, who heals all your diseases, who redeems your life from the pit, who crowns you with steadfast love and mercy, who satisfies you with good as long as you live, so that your youth is renewed like the eagle's."

David's Psalm is a statement of heartfelt thanksgiving for God's goodness that He has prepared for us to receive as His precious humankind. He details how God blesses us, our very souls. If we are freed up from sins by the acceptance of Jesus as our Savior, how then did we not see and believe that God loves us? It is the grace of God that gives us true victory in this life and for eternity!

You can only rely on your efforts and your willpower for so long and they can only bring you so far. We need to put our dependency completely on the Lord's grace. That grace will set you free to more completely follow in His pathway. This is the good news. The more we hear and practice it, the more God extends grace to us! The Book of Acts declares that where there is great grace, there is great steadfast love.

OCTOBER 28
SCRIPTURE: EPHESIANS 4:26–27 (TEV)

"If you become angry, do not let your anger lead you into sin, and do not stay angry all day. Don't give the Devil a chance."

Anger may be one of the devil's most dangerous and often used temptation to move us toward acts of sin. When anger is carried to its fullest degree it becomes hate. Anger is a feeling of displeasure or hostility that one feels when another injures, mistrusts, or opposes you. Anger then increases your feelings, actions, words to hate, which is a stronger feeling of anger. These actions can be directed toward you or be directed from you. Anger must be resolved before the feeling becomes hate!

In working toward resolution of your anger issues (and we all have them), you may want to enlist help from: the Holy Trinity, family, a friend, a pastor, another believer, or professional counseling. May the peace and love and forgiveness of the Lord be with you now and forever.

OCTOBER 29
SCRIPTURE: MATTHEW 5:14 & 15 (NRSV)

"You are the light of the world. Let your light shine before others, so that they may see your works and give glory to your Father in Heaven."

Immediately after Jesus taught the beatitudes in the fifth chapter of Matthew, He focused on light and letting our light shine on others. Think about this expression: "You can read someone like a book." Each of us could be the first exposure that someone has heard about the Lord. From that experience the person may want to hear more or they may go in the other direction. You see, that person may have read you like a book! Remember, Jesus passed the torch of His spiritual offering when He tells us in the scripture above, "Let your light shine before men." This command places a great responsibility on us as believers. Jesus moved on from this earth and we are to spiritually step into action. Our words, our actions, and our deeds may be under scrutiny and we may not even know about it! In the love chapter of the New Testament (1 Corinthians 13:13) Paul tells us, "These three remain: faith, hope, and love." Our single source for acquiring these characteristics is Jesus Himself. Let your "Christ-likeness" be read by others.

OCTOBER 30
SCRIPTURE: PSALM 13:1–3 (NRSV)

"How long, O Lord? Will you forget me forever? How long, will you hide your face from me? How long must I bear pain in my soul and have sorrow in my heart all day long? How long shall my enemy be exalted over me?"

Do you ever question God? It seems apparent that the Bible, especially the Book of Psalms, includes detailed accounts of God's people who were sorely disappointed with God. They apparently sought to bring to God most every emotional and spiritual event in their daily activities. They were trying to obey all of God's laws. They learned the hard way that the law did not bring them forgiveness, joy, or peace. The author Philip Yancey writes this about questioning God: "It may seem strange for sacred writings to include such scenes of spiritual failures." We know that God wants what is best for His people. Wrongdoing on our part needs to be exposed before understanding and healing can occur. Could it be that questioning God may actually provide the beginning of healing?

OCTOBER 31
SCRIPTURE: JAMES 1:21 (NRSV)

"Therefore rid yourselves of all sordidness and rank growth of wickedness, and welcome with meekness the implanted word that has the power to save your souls."

One of God's earliest covenants with His people was to write them on stone (the Ten Commandments). In Exodus 24:12-14 God said, "I will give you tables of stone, with the law and commandments which I have written for their instruction." These commandments were referred to frequently in the Old Testament. But as we know the people did not, as we do not today, follow them. So by the time of Jeremiah in the seventh century, God changed His approach to communicate with His people. In Jeremiah 31:31, God stated, "I will put my law within them and write it on their hearts."

So God moved from the external writings on the stone tablets to the internal, built-in function of the heart. Hear again God's words: "welcome with meekness that has the power to save your souls." This is where we find ourselves today, with His implanted words in our souls. However, we know, even today, that we often disregard God's desire for us. But the reason for our disobedience is our failure, not God's! We cannot save our own soul. But God can!

NOVEMBER 1
SCRIPTURE: EPHESIANS 2:8–10 (NRSV)

"Faith is the gift of God, not the result of works, so that no one may boast. For we are what He has made us, created in Christ Jesus for good works, which God prepared before-hand to be our way of life."

Recently, I read this sentence: "Get your good going!" I decided to see if I could find an example in the Bible of this sentence. You can see in the above scripture that I succeeded. A good illustration was our scripture above, which speaks of good works that are motivated by God's gift of faith in union with Jesus. It also tells us that our good works are to be our way of life, since God has already prepared them for us.

An often used term that we hear today is "do-gooder." A do-gooder is an idealist, but impractical person who seeks to correct social ills. These people can be effective, honorable, virtuous, and kind. But they many times are seeking recognition for themselves, and if it helps others, so be it! James 4:17 says, "So then, the person who does not do the good he knows he should do is guilty of sin. Get your "good going" according to what Christ dictates to you!

NOVEMBER 2
SCRIPTURE: PSALM 23:4 (NRSV)

"Even though I walk through the darkest valley, I fear no evil; for you are with me; your rod and your staff—they comfort me."

I read that the popular band The Eagles practice their music and harmony by sitting in a circle to perfect their presentation. In that small circle, they can immediately recognize their mistakes. They continue their practice with the error being corrected by the individual who made the mistake. Once corrected, the group continues with almost perfection in their music. Two interesting actions occur within their system. First, the group does not dismiss the offender, and they jointly replay the arrangement.

Their technique brings about their splendid music both instrumentally and vocally. Their actions bring about a sense of absolute exposure and from a musical standpoint. It could also represent exposure of sin from our standpoint. It also represents the method of forgiveness of sin. There is no place to hide and no way to hide our sin from God Almighty.

NOVEMBER 3
SCRIPTURE: JOHN 13:35 (TEV)

"If you have love for one another, then everyone will know that you are
my disciples.

When I was a little boy there was a kind, gentle man who talked to himself while
he worked. I could never hear him but I could see his lips moving frequently. I
was told that he was repeating to himself the memorized material that he had to
learn and repeat as a member of a fraternal organization to which he belonged.
As he rose in rank in that organization, he had to memorize more and more
and he talked to himself more and more. He succeeded in this group because
he could repeat memorized paragraphs almost perfectly. Isn't it great that we
don't have to go through some repetitive act or structured presentations to
demonstrate our Christian faith. All we have to do, according to Jesus, is to
have love for one another. All it costs us "to have" that love is to be free from
our own selfishness and pride…free to accept God's gift and to pass it on in our
relationships with others. We don't need membership, creeds, organizations,
etc. We just need love for our fellow human beings. Practice this act of love and
the world will know that we are His people.

NOVEMBER 4
SCRIPTURE: GENESIS 3:9–10 (TEV)

"But the Lord God called out to Adam, 'Where are you?' He answered, 'I heard you in the garden; I was afraid and hid from you, because I was naked.'"

Fear is defined by Webster's dictionary as anxiety caused by real or possible danger, pain, etc. In the *Strong's Concise Concordance*, the word *fear* or a derivation of the word is used 521 times. That fact probably means that anxiety-producing fear has been in action since the creation of humankind. In the Garden of Eden, when Adam answered God's question, he replied, "I was afraid and hid from you." Adam feared God because he had been disobedient to God! Adam sinned against God! Unfortunately, sin has existed even until today. And it will continue until the end of the age. We have all experienced fear…we have observed fear in others. Fear causes different reactions from each of us, depending on a large degree on how we perceive the action and the consequence of the action. The psalmist in 34:4 states, "I prayed to the Lord, and He answered me; He freed me from all my fears." I know of no better advice for us to follow than to pray!

NOVEMBER 5
SCRIPTURE: MATTHEW 13:10–11 (TEV)

"Then the disciples came up to Jesus and asked Him, 'Why do you use parables when you talk to the people?' Jesus answered, 'the knowledge about the secrets of the kingdom of heaven has been given to you, but not to them.'"

Jesus used parables as a teaching method, as did the prophets of the Old Testament. His ultimate purpose was and is to establish His kingdom and the reign of heaven in the hearts of humankind. The Jews felt that the kingdom of God was an exclusive blessing for the Jewish people only. Just in Matthew 13, Jesus told the people in many parables about: the kingdom, service and obedience, prayer, neighbors, humility, wealth, God's love, thankfulness, judgment, and the future. The disciples understood most of Jesus' parables because they were committed to Jesus' ministry and purpose. His parables made the truth clearer and more understandable because of the common, well-accepted words and ideas that were known to the people. His teachings, through the use of parables, are as valuable to us today as they were to the believers and people of His time.

NOVEMBER 6
SCRIPTURE: 11 PETER 1:3 (TEV)

"God's divine power has given us everything we need to live a Godly life through our knowledge of the one who called us to share His own glory and goodness."

Peter is writing to believers who have obtained precious faith. His writings are as true and valuable to us today as to the people of his time. Christians should see that we have the promise of future life and He wants us to abide in Christian values. God's word states that the process is in His divine power; that God may bestow His power as He pleases; that we cannot refute His purpose, to bestow His righteousness upon us; and that it is His favor that we can only obtain from Him. This constitutes the basis of our hopes of becoming partakers of the divine nature of God.

NOVEMBER 7
SCRIPTURE: PSALM 32:1–2 (TEV)

"Happy are those whose sins are forgiven, whose wrongs are pardoned. Happy is the man whom the Lord does not accuse of doing wrong and who is free from all deceit."

The Book of Psalms presents us with great scripture regarding repentance and forgiveness. Collectively, the Psalms give us these reasons for reading them: to find comfort, to meet God intimately, to learn to pray more productively, to give thanks to God, and to know why we should worship God. God's word was written for us to reap, study, understand, and to be applied in our own lives. They put into words our deepest hurts, longings, thoughts, and prayers. They gently push us toward what God created us to be—people loving, worshipping, and living for Him. Over the years, many believers who have been burdened by their own sins have found the words of Psalms as rays of hope. God responds to our repentance with His forgiveness. Praise God!

NOVEMBER 8
SCRIPTURE: JOEL 2:12–13 (TEV)

"But even now, says the Lord, repent sincerely and return to me…. Let your broken heart show your sorrow…. Come back to the Lord your God. He is kind and full of mercy; He is patient and keeps His promise. He is always ready to forgive and not punish."

Remember, as far back as the Prophet, God made this proclamation: "I was always ready to answer, 'Here I am; I will help you!'" These same words assure us this day. God wants us to be committed to His word. Best of all, He will help. If God is for us, who can be against us? Have great expectations of God Almighty as you make your requests through prayers.

NOVEMBER 9
SCRIPTURE: LUKE 24:27 (NRSV)

"Then beginning with Moses and all the Prophets, Jesus, interpreted to them the things about Himself in all the scriptures."

Jesus often challenged the prevailing interpretations of scripture, calling for His listeners to move from the letter of the law to the spirit of the law. We know today that it is necessary to read and study God's word, to be obedient to God, and to receive His grace. It is God's plan for us to have a soul-saving experience with Jesus. This experience comes quickly for some, more slowly for some, and for some the encounter never comes. It is our responsibility to deepen our knowledge and love of the Lord if we are to receive that encounter because Jesus has said, "I will never turn anyone away, who comes to me." Reading and studying the scriptures does not require us to be theologians or Bible historians, but rather to be disciplined, serious, and motivated to learn about Jesus.

NOVEMBER 10
SCRIPTURE: 11 PETER 1:16 AND 18 (NRSV)

"For we did not follow cleverly devised myths when we made known to you the power and coming of our Lord Jesus Christ, but we had been eye witnesses of His majesty. We ourselves heard this voice come from heaven, while we were with Jesus on the holy mountain."

Peter seems to have been a natural leader; and if you will notice of Jesus' disciples, Peter's name is usually listed first. Peter is not tooting his own horn in the above scripture; he is attempting to validate his personal knowledge of being with Jesus and hearing God's voice. That makes Peter one to listen to, even in our day. Peter was stressing to the people of his day (and to us) what he had seen and heard. Later in the scripture, Peter reminds us to let the rising of the morning star occur in our hearts. In fact, Jesus Himself, in Revelation 22:16, proclaims, "I am the root and branch of David, the bright morning star." Let us move forward and spiritually to be lifted by the rising of Jesus (the morning star) in our lives.

"So then, as the body without the spirit is dead, also faith without actions and works is dead."

What does the Bible say about faith and works? Hebrew 11:1-4 states "to have faith is to be sure of things we hope for, to be certain of the things we cannot see." It was by faith that the people of ancient times won God's approval. Faith gives us the force of reality to believe. We do not see God, or heaven, or angels, or the crown of Glory, but we have faith in them. This then leads us to act as if we saw them. Look now at spiritual works. In Ephesians 2:10, it is written, in union with Christ Jesus, God has created us for a life of good deeds (works), which He has already prepared for us to do." The good works are already here for us to do! But for God's plan to work, we must have both, faith and works. Spiritually, one does not exist without the other.

NOVEMBER 12
SCRIPTURE: JEREMIAH 29:12-13 (TEV)

"Then you will call to me. You will come and pray to me, and I will answer you. You will seek me, and you will find me because you will seek me with all your heart."

The Israelites were, at that time, in exile (or disconnected) from God and their homeland. The Prophet Jeremiah warned God's people of the catastrophic circumstances of their failure to follow God's leading, but they did not listen. Today, one denomination in the U.S. states, "we deserve God's condemnation!" However, as with the exiles of the Old Testament, God says to us, "I will let you find me." He wants what is best for us, and He restores us when we come back to Him with repentant hearts. And He lets us find Him!! If we take a reality check in our time, we find that we live in disturbing times; as a nation, as a people, and as individuals. As individuals, we find that we are disconnected from the Lord and are not in union with Him. The Bible tells us that God said, "I was always ready to say, I will help you!" The question for each of us is this: How do we seek and find God? We must: repent, confess, accept forgiveness, and change our lifestyle and strive to live a Christ-like life!

NOVEMBER 13
SCRIPTURE: PSALM 5:9-10 (NRSV)

"Hide your face from my sins, and blot out all my iniquities. Create in me a clean heart, O God, and put a new and right spirit within me."

We don't have to live long before we realize that our words and/or our actions are very capable of causing hurt to others. There are times when we have longed to undo, do over, or take back a word, an action, a choice, or a moment. A time when we should have held our tongue, but instead spoke harsh, wounding words to someone; a time when we should have spoken the truth, but remained silent; a time when we said yes, rather than saying no; a time when we turned away, instead of turning toward. Those times are over!! We can't do them over but we can seek God's forgiveness through our repentance and prayer. God will still love us enough to re-establish our relation of love with Him! We can start over with His faithfulness. No rewind button is needed.

NOVEMBER 14
SCRIPTURE: 2 TIMOTHY 3:15 (NRSV)

"From childhood you have known the sacred writings that are able to instruct you for salvation through faith in Christ Jesus."

You may not have had the opportunity to be exposed to the sacred word (Bible) since childhood. However, it's not too late; you can start this very day. We live in troubled times, especially with moral issues of today. How do we handle the issues of our time? The Holy Bible, according to the above scripture, the sacred writings are able to instruct you. The scripture can enhance our strength as we gain faith and wisdom from reading and studying God's word. This scripture indicates that all scripture, not necessarily one or two verses, not one or two chapters, not one or two books, not just the Old Testament, not just the New Testament! No! All scripture, all of God's words, are available for us in many verses. Who can argue with the truth and grace of the words "inspired by Almighty God"? Try it today!

NOVEMBER 15
SCRIPTURE: HEBREWS 4:14 (NRSV)

"Since then, we have a great high priest who has passed through the heavens, Jesus, the son of God. Let us therefore approach the throne of grace with boldness, so that we may receive mercy and find grace to help in time of need."

It appears that the writer of Hebrews' attempts to demonstrate God's movement from the Old to the New Testaments was to show His plan of salvation through His son, Jesus Christ. The relation between Christianity and Judaism was a critical issue in the development of the early church. His message (writer of Hebrews) was extremely difficult for the Jews to accept, although they had sought the Messiah for centuries. They were entrenched in their thinking and worship in the old traditional ways.

Thus, the writers of the New Testament and the founders of the early church had to describe God's promises and to reveal the way to forgiveness and salvation through God's son, Jesus Christ, whom they could not accept. All that the Lord needed from humankind was the sacrifice of a contrite and grateful heart. All that was needed on the part of God was to provide a way of salvation that had been done through Jesus. All that remains for humankind is to forsake their sins and go back to a God who wants to be forgiving and gracious.

NOVEMBER 16
SCRIPTURE: GENESIS 1:1 (NRSV)

"In the beginning God."

These four words introduce us to the Holy Bible. The words set the direction for everything that comes after in the drama of creation. The pathway for life, our life, is clearly demonstrated for us by the commands, the directions, and the guidance of the Holy Trinity. The Bible presents us God, the Creator; Jesus, the Savior; and the Holy Spirit, the indwelling counselor. We need to understand that was and is the very beginning of all things and that humankind was and is at the top of His creation. He was and is forever desiring what is best for us. He intends for His precious humankind to live out our earthly journey well.

Someone told me this acronym about the Bible: Basic Instruction Before Leaving Earth. This is what we need to remember before we make choices, examining the Trinity's directions for our actions, by recognizing that the Christ-like life is the way to eternal life. Pray, read, understand, and respond according to God's word, the Bible.

NOVEMBER 17
SCRIPTURE: MATTHEW 7:28–29 (TEV)

"When Jesus finished saying these things (from His Sermon on the Mount) the crowd was amazed at the way He taught. He wasn't like the teachers of the law: instead, He taught with authority."

The reason the people "were amazed at the way He taught" was that His teachings were taught with the authority of God. Before this Sermon on the Mount, the people only heard the teaching of the religious leaders of that time who taught based on the law. The law had its purpose; it was the traditional religious aspects of the day. Jesus knew that the Father God wanted the people to follow His way and seek redemption through His plan of salvation. That is what Jesus was teaching. His teachings were a threat to the traditional teachings of that time, and eventually brought about the death of Jesus. However, as John stated in 1:5, "The light shines in the darkness, and the darkness did not overcome it." The light still shines some two thousand years later. God still wants us to follow His plan of salvation taught to us in the Bible. "Let Him who has ears listen."

NOVEMBER 18
SCRIPTURE: EPHESIANS 2:10 (TEV)

"God has made us what we are, and in our union with Christ Jesus He has created us for a life of good deeds, which He has already prepared for us to do."

This verse confirms that "God has made us what we are." Examine your own fingertips: You are looking at fingerprints unlike any other person in His image… recipients of His gifts. As remarkable as humankind is, we still do not reach our full expectation of God until we are "in union with Christ Jesus." Then God's precious mankind is joined by His only begotten Son, and together we are to enjoy a life of good deeds. Now we are ready; we need only to be sensitive to the needs of others. Be sure, God has already planned for us to become involved.

NOVEMBER 19
SCRIPTURE: 2 CORINTHIANS 12:9 (NRSV)

"My grace is all you need, for my power is greatest when you are weak!"

In this scripture, the Lord told Paul the solution to deal with his brokenness. Does that statement really make sense to you? And what about Paul's response? He says, "I am most happy, then, to be proud of my weakness!" Obviously, this conversation was based on a spiritual level, brought about by total surrender of self to the healing power of God's grace. On the surface, God's statement seeks to be in direction to the American's mind-set of what an individual is taught (and cultivated by society). The process of "pulling one's self up by their own bootstraps." You see, God's grace leads us through most of our lives when we have experienced Jesus Christ as our personal savior. God does not promise us a light load through our lives. In fact, sometimes our loads are very heavy; sometimes hardship stoops our shoulders, slows our steps, and robs our sleep. God does not promise to insulate us from burdens and exempt us from pain and sorrow. However, He does promise to always be with us! Remember the Lord's statement from the last verse of the Book of Matthews. "I will be with you always, to the end of the age."

NOVEMBER 20
SCRIPTURE: PSALM 23:4 (NRSV)

"Yea, though I walk through the valley of the shadow of death, I will fear no evil, for you are with me."

Notice, the scripture does not say I do not die there or stop there…but rather, "I walk through the valley." The psalmist's walk is in the shadow of death, not the valley of death. There is a definite difference. For the believer, the valley of the shadow of death is not an end, but merely the door into a higher and more exalted and intimate life with the Lord. It is not something to fear, but an experience through which one passes on the path to a more perfect life to come. With this conviction, the believer moves onto a higher ground with God. Knowing Him in this manner makes life before death much more bearable for the Christian.

Life and death in nature are not the subject, but rather death and life in Christ should be our focus. Death to the nonbeliever perhaps offers an endless time in a state where God is not present. In short, the Bible promises life through death. And we should celebrate coming out on the other side of the valley!

NOVEMBER 21
SCRIPTURE: JOSHUA 24:13-14 (NRSV)

"I gave you a land on which you had not labored. And towns that you had not built, and you lived in them; you ate the fruit of vineyards and olive yards that you did not plant. Now, therefore, revere the Lord, and serve Him in sincerity and in faithfulness."

In this scripture, the Lord is speaking through Joshua and asking the people to review God's part in Israel's long history up to that time. Basically God is telling them to review, to remember, and to renew His goodness bestowed upon them. When we consider our own nation, especially at our time of Thanksgiving, it is well for us to include in our thanks and appreciation to God Almighty. In so doing, we should review our blessings; we should remember our heritage; and we should renew our faith and hope. It would not hurt us to consider these same points about our own lives. It would be a good assignment for each of us to count our many blessings during these troubled times. We still need to remember often our nation's motto, "One nation under God!"

NOVEMBER 22
SCRIPTURE: JAMES 1:19 (NRSV)

"You must understand this, my beloved, let everyone be quick to listen, slow to speak, slow to anger. For your anger does not produce God's righteousness."

Those who study the behavior of humankind tell us that in every culture, humans seek someone or something to worship. Why is this? Because God has written it in our hearts. So James explains what is required of us by way of responses; meekness. How then does meekness express itself? It involves: "quick to listen" (being a good listener); "slow to speak" (being thoughtful and deliberate); and "slow to anger" (not overly hasty and given to jumping to conclusions). We need to be willing to go into action when wrong is shown to be one's own account.

We complicate matters by our own desire to have our point made, accepted, and acted upon. The Holy Spirit which indwells within us empowers us to proclaim as Romans 8 states: "God's spirit joins Himself to our spirit to declare that we are God's children." Call on the Holy Spirit to empower you to do God's will.

NOVEMBER 23
SCRIPTURE: JAMES 3:17 (TEV)

"The wisdom from above is pure. First of all; it is also peaceful, gentle, and friendly; it is full of compassion and produces a harvest of good deeds; it is free from prejudice and hypocrisy."

The above scripture is written by James as a collection of practical instruction to God's people scattered over the world (known at that time). These instructions are regarding wisdom and knowledge. Knowledge is a body of facts that are learned by an individual and could be referred to as earthly knowledge. Those who claimed to have earthly knowledge had not experienced Jesus Christ in their lives. However, wisdom as explained by James were those people who knew Jesus by personal experience and who possessed those qualities that James listed in the above scripture. Proverbs, 4:7-8, says, "getting wisdom is the most important thing you can do. Love wisdom and she will make you great. Embrace her, and she will bring you honor. She will be your crowning glory." Let the Lord fill you with His wisdom.

NOVEMBER 24
SCRIPTURE: 2 CORINTHIANS 8:12 (TEV)

"If you are eager to give, God will accept your gift on the basis of what you have to give, not on what you don't have."

In giving to God, we must first remember that God does not actually need anything that we can give Him. His completeness is not increased by anything that we can give Him. However, he does accept and that acceptance is generosity beyond our comprehension. In this verse, it would appear that the expectation is to give, based on this criteria: our eagerness to give and what we have to give. The eagerness is an attitude or mind-set, which generally reflects compassion, positive thinking, selflessness, praise, thanksgiving…something you want to share out of your realization of who God is and who He is to you. The second element would seem to be a gift of some kind. Perhaps something in the categories of money, time, talent, or service. You see, these are gifts that He has already given to each of us, in varying degrees and portions… and all that He wants is to accept what you can give, not what you can't give. Remember, one of the Proverbs says, "When you give to the poor, it is like lending to the Lord, and the Lord will pay you back." (Proverbs 19:17). That being the case, I doubt that you could ever give away all of your love.

NOVEMBER 25
SCRIPTURE: EXODUS 34:6 (TEV)

"I, the Lord, am a God who is full of compassion and pity."

Compassion is defined as the sympathetic consciousness of other's distress with a desire to alleviate it. Because this was the nature and character of their God, the Prophets declared that compassion was one of the essentials of membership in their community. All who know God and who call themselves His children must cultivate and show compassion in their lives. We need to make a distinction between a person who is compassionate and the person who is a "do-gooder." Compassion is a God-given gift. A do-gooder creates an act that usually brings more satisfaction to the giver than to the receiver of the action.

When God instills us with compassion, He makes us a blessing so that we can be a blessing to others. We don't have to create compassion; we just have to be open for compassion to flood our hearts.

NOVEMBER 26
SCRIPTURE: I TIMOTHY 1:5 (PHILLIPS VERSION)

"The ultimate aim of the Christian ministry, after all, is to arouse the love which springs from a pure heart, a good conscience, and a genuine faith."

The Bible tells us that God is love. He also wants to have a love relationship with us. Then He created in man the capacity to love one another. That capacity is built in us and is ready to respond when our feeling and/or needs are aroused to seek God. Even though the capacity is there, it does not function automatically. It's like a fire in that it does not ignite of its own volition…it requires a spark, a match, lightning, or some other source to begin to burn. In the scripture above, Paul is telling Timothy that he must, to be effective in his ministry, simply arouse love in people and to move them toward the Lord.

Paul also suggests to Timothy that he must cultivate his own love of God so that he can win souls. The arousal of love will then come through Timothy and it will spring from his "pure heart, a good conscience, and genuine faith." Charles Spurgeon said, "a pure heart created by God is to be seen everywhere." Let your love shine today!

NOVEMBER 27
SCRIPTURE: MARK 7:6–7 (TEV)

"These people (Pharisees), says God, honor me with their words, but their hearts are really far away from me. It is no use for them to worship me, because they teach man-made rules as though they were my laws! You put aside God's command, and obey the teachings of men."

In the message version of the Bible, the subheading for chapter 7 of Mark is entitled "The source of your pollution." Then it is indicated that the source of human's pollution is the heart. So, we experience two types of pollution in our world today...namely pollution of the environment and pollution of our hearts. Jesus tells the Pharisees who were trying to "trap" Jesus by pointing out that the disciples were eating their meals without washing their hands. Then Jesus pointed out that the religious present at that time were attempting "to teach man-made rules as though they were God's Laws." Maybe we all can admit to pollution of our hearts at times. But the religious leaders of Jesus' time would say that our ways are not polluted. But that's exactly what they taught. They trained themselves to strictly observe their traditions, which were man-made. God wants us to faithfully be obedient to His word and His laws.

NOVEMBER 28
SCRIPTURE: MARK 5:18-20 (NRSV)

"As Jesus was getting into the boat, Legion the man who had been possessed by demons, begged Him that He might be with Jesus. But Jesus refused, and said to him, 'Go home to your friends, and tell them how much the Lord has done for you, and what mercy He has shown you.' And he went away and began to proclaim in the Decapolis how much Jesus had done for him; and everyone was amazed."

Legion was the demonic man who could not be bound by chains and who ran wild in a cemetery. Jesus instructed the saved Legion to go and tell what the Lord had done for him. Jesus wanted him to share his story. Legion obeyed Jesus and became one of the first missionaries to tell of Jesus' power and concern.

Not only did Legion go home and tell his friends, he went to the area known as the Decapolis, which was actually ten separate communities.

My own personal experience with the Lord was akin to Legion's story. I left my office on Friday and returned to work on Monday as a saved man. I had a saving experience with Jesus. I was sharing "my story" with anyone who would listen. I heard some of the staff members whispering in low voices, "Something has happened to Charles. He's talking so much about the Lord." And I was!! I was so happy with my newfound Lord that I felt compelled to share the news with my whole staff, one at a time.

"You desire truth in the inward being; therefore, teach me wisdom in my secret heart."

One Sunday morning when participating in a responsive reading from the fifty-first Psalm, this phrase, "Teach me wisdom in my secret heart," leaped from the pages of the hymn book into my mind. In almost indelible fashion, the phrase has remained with me...as if mysteriously seeking closer scrutiny. Still, the words remain, clinging at first, then slowly encompassing a larger, more sensitive section of my inner being...my own secret heart, as it were.

Each of us has this place where we receive God's will and work through our response to His will. That sounds uncomplicated; however, we know that this process is not easy, not even conscious for some. Too often, we think with all our knowledge and expertise, that we can gain wisdom without Him. But the wisdom we desire in our secret hearts is unattainable without God. This is verified by a startling scriptural fact found in I Corinthians 1:21; which states, "For God in His wisdom made it impossible for people to know Him by means of their own wisdom." But even more revealing and reassuring for our seeking, secret hearts is this proclamation that follows in verse 24: "This message is Christ, who is the power of God and the wisdom of God." Wisdom is no longer cloaked in mystery, no longer unavailable for my secret heart...God fleshes it out in the person of Jesus Christ.

Do you know this Jesus in your secret heart?

NOVEMBER 30
SCRIPTURE: EPHESIANS 2:10 (THE MESSAGE)

"We neither make nor save ourselves. God does both the making and saving. He creates each of us by Christ Jesus to join Him in the work He does, the good work He has gotten ready for us to do. Work we had better be doing."

We recognize some of the difficulties that we sometimes experience in verbal expression. If that creates problems for us, we need to focus on communication by which both our actions and/or deeds affect others. Expressing our testimony invites this question: Can others tell that you are indeed a child of God? When we experience Jesus Christ, we become representatives of the Lord by assuming to do His work. We were given the awesome responsibility of reflecting God's love, mercy, and grace. The last phrase in the scripture above is critical that we understand: "work we had better be doing!"

Remember when we do God's works, we glorify our Father in heaven! We do not do those works to show how good we are. We are thankful to God, and we want to act as His representatives; that being the case, participation in good works may be our best method of testimony. Others watch our way of living much more than our way of speaking.

DECEMBER 1
SCRIPTURE: EXODUS 3:11–12 (TEV)

"But Moses said to God, 'I am nobody. How can I go to the king and bring the Israelites out of Egypt.' God answered, 'I will be with you and when you bring the people out of Egypt, you will worship me on this mountain.'

The Old Testament scripture reminds us often of God's frequent place of being found is on a mountain. Such is the place where He instructs Moses to return from Egypt to worship Him "on this mountain." It seems that one would likely go upon a mountain to make a loud, clear proclamation to others in a group. We have probably never used such a technique for an announcement. We don't really need to go to that distance of communicating a message. Have you ever told another about Jesus? You know that telling of your experience with Him may be just as effective as that of biblical characters. We can share our own story with others. We can share our experience in our own way, using our own method. Matthew 28:20 tells us that Jesus, speaking to His disciples, says, "And I will be with you always, to the end of the age." Perhaps we could use the words of this spiritual song to share the message of God:

> "Go tell it on the mountain,
> Over the hills and everywhere;
> Go tell it on the mountain,
> That Jesus Christ is born."
> (author unknown)

DECEMBER 2
SCRIPTURE: PSALM 51:10–11 (NRSV)

"Create in me a clean heart, O God, and put a new and right spirit within me. Do not cast me away from your presence, and do not take your Holy Spirit from me."

After the Prophet Nathan had confronted David about David's adultery with Bathsheba, he prayed to God, admitting his sin and requesting God's forgiveness. God made all of His precious humankind to be able to feel guilt and separation from God. We all have sinned against Him, our families, our friends, and others; we all have that inner knowledge that we have wronged Him. And that feeling of guilt does not go away, unless and until we have admitted the sin and asked Him for forgiveness. We do not find rest and peace until we seek forgiveness. We may think that we have hidden the sin from God, but we only fool ourselves—God always knows about us!

DECEMBER 3
SCRIPTURE: MATTHEW 8:2-3 (NRSV)

"Then a man suffering from a dreaded skin disease came to Jesus, knelt down before Him, and said, 'Sir, if you want to, you can make me clean!' Jesus reached out and touched him. 'I do want to,' He answered! 'Be Clean!' At once the man was healed of his disease."

Jesus' three main aspects of His ministry were preaching, teaching, and healing. This devotion is focused on His healings. These acts indicate the real power of His 'touch of the Master's hand.' They demonstrate His concern for wellness and wholeness; His concern for commitment. The touch also authenticated His preaching and teaching, proving that He was truly from God. There are other scriptures in the Gospels that indicate the healing power of Jesus' touch. Christ can also heal us of spiritual sickness as well as physical ailments. His touch, His words, His concern, and His compassion all offer to us freedom, hope, peace, and eternal life.

I do not personally know anyone who has the gift of healing. However, there are many people who have a comforting touch, which I believe most of us can use effectively with hurting people. Let me share the following ideas for you to have a comforting hand to those whom you want to help but don't know what you can do. Be there; it's not easy to see a suffering person or friend. Maybe you would rather not see them. Remember, being there may mean more than your words. Hold their hand or touch them if it is appropriate. Listen to them. Let them set the agenda for the conversation. You may not have the right answer. Don't be afraid of tears; let them cry if they want to, and it's okay for you to cry. Also, Jesus stated to His disciples these instructions: "Do as your teacher." Jesus wouldn't mind if you also followed His example of touching and comforting and loving! (from an article in a magazine, *Modern Maturity*, December 1988)

DECEMBER 4
SCRIPTURE: ISAIAH 11: 1–2 (TEV)

"A new king will arise from among David's descendants. The spirit of the Lord will give Him wisdom and the knowledge and skill to rule His people. He will know the Lord's will and will have reverence for Him, and find pleasure in obeying Him."

Advent was a time of preparing to welcome again God's gift of love shown in Jesus Christ. This occasion had been expected by the Israelite people for centuries. They longed for the Messiah in sincere anticipation for His coming. Christians now celebrate the season of advent for the four Sundays in December preceding Christmas Day. Isaiah continues in verse 9, same chapter, "The land will be as full of knowledge of the Lord as the seas are full of water." The Messiah was Jesus, and His coming changed the world forever!

DECEMBER 5
SCRIPTURE: 2 PETER 1–4 (TEV)

"God's divine power has given us everything we need to live a truly religious life. You may be called to share His divine nature."

God has provided and remained faithful to these promises:

Since creation, namely the following:

> God's creation of humankind
> God's creation of nature
> God's selection of His people
> God's plan for His people
> God's protection of His people
> God's direction for His people
> God's prophets who told of the coming of the Messiah
> in the New Testament:
> God gave His only son to the world as a gift
> God gave His Holy Spirit to the people
> God gave us the way to make things right with Him

Through Jesus' preachings, teachings, and healings, believers began to look beyond themselves to reach out to others to share the spiritual gifts freely given to us by God. The believers of Jesus' time (and believers of our time) are sent all over the world to spread the word to others.

In this sense, we too are able to be God-sent into the world to reflect the very divine nature of the Lord. Today, the majority of His people stay at home, go to church, love each other, and give of their funds. In giving of their funds (which are necessary) they are satisfied with just "sending" their funds to support projects for the less fortunate in this country and in foreign countries. The challenge for the church today is to become more missional in our own churches and communities. The Lord still desires God-sent believers to be about His work locally as well as worldwide.

DECEMBER 6
SCRIPTURE: ISAIAH 30:19–21 (TEV)

"The Lord is compassionate, and when you cry to Him for help, He will answer you. The Lord will make you go through hard times, but He Himself will be there to teach you, and you will not have to search for Him anymore. If you wander off the road to the right or the left, You will hear His voice behind you saying, 'Here is the road, follow it.'"

"If you wander off the road!" The key word in this phrase above is 'wander!' I am almost one hundred percent sure that everyone who reads this devotion has wandered in their spiritual journey in life. The definition is "to go astray in mind or purpose." The Bible shares with us countless numbers of those who have wandered from the way. In fact, the whole nation of Israel wandered in the wilderness for forty years before going into the promised land. Wandering is so human that we sometimes aren't even aware that we erred in our actions. Apparently, we at times do not obey the Lord's voice, saying, "Here is the road; follow it!" The good news is that the faithful Lord will still help you. Robert Robinson in his hymn "Come Thou Fount of Every Blessing" writes this in one of the stanzas: "Prone to wander, Lord I feel it, prone to leave the God I love." The actions of one's wandering have been with people since the beginning of time. And God has been there to direct us back to the way when we seek Him with our heartfelt request. Listen for His directions!

DECEMBER 7
SCRIPTURE: PSALM 30:10–12 (TEV)

"Hear me, Lord, and be merciful! Help me Lord! You have changed my sadness into a joyful dance; you have taken away my sorrow and surrounded me with joy. So I will not be silent; I will sing praise to you. Lord, you are my God; I will give you thanks forever."

"Be all you can be" was a slogan used in an advertisement by the U.S. Army. In the above scripture by King David, you can almost feel some of his excitement, joy, and thanksgiving as he expresses his true feelings to the Lord. This feeling filled him as he rejoices that the Lord had answered his request for help. His response for the Lord's help? "I will give you thanks forever." He states that he "will not be silent." We are God's people and upon conversion we can be so much more for God, others, and ourselves. Choose the Lord today and "Be all you can be!"

DECEMBER 8
SCRIPTURE: MATTHEW 8:26-27 (NRSV)

"Then He got up and rebuked the winds and the sea; and there was dead calm."

The movement of water in a pond, a lake, a river, or the sea has always intrigued me. A number of years ago, a Simon and Garfunkel song entitled "Bridge Over Troubled Waters" was very popular. It was a beautiful love song in which the man offered, when his lover experienced "trouble waters in her life, to lay himself down over the trouble as a bridge. This would allow the lady to cross over the trouble with less difficulty and allow the man to express his love. The song presents two ideas: one, of troubled times in our lives, and two, bridging those troubles to reduce the pain of such. Generally, the movement of bodies of water can be found in still water, ripples in the water, white caps on the water, or storms upon the water. In any case, if one is to cross troubled waters, a bridge is often required.

These four conditions of water can parallel trouble in our lives, and we all have experienced such. For our spiritual wellness, we need a bridge over troubled waters. I think back to bridges of my youth, which were usually constructed of wooden planks or boards. Perhaps I can use the idea of planks to suggest how we might construct a bridge that will allow a crossing over the troubles in our lives. We need "spiritual" planks for this event. Let me suggest these possible solutions. Let your planks be represented by: family, friends, and the Lord. Family is where God starts our lives and surrounds us with love, concern, support, and nurture. Friends demonstrate a different kind of love; they choose us to love, unlike the family in which we are born. The Lord said, "when anyone is joined to Christ, that person is a new being; the old is gone, the new has come." See these "planks" when you are faced with troubled waters.

DECEMBER 9
SCRIPTURE: JONAH 1:2 (TEV)

"One day the Lord spoke to Jonah. He said, 'Go to Nineveh, that great city, and speak out against it; I am aware of how wicked its people are.'"

Jonah was a prophet of the Lord who disobeyed the Lord by initially refusing to take God's message to the sinful city of Nineveh. So He went in the other direction, by boat, "to get away from the Lord's calling." We tend, when considering this book, to focus on the whole story rather than the example of God's faithful forgiveness. For you see, Jonah, when he felt the realization that he was about to die in the stomach of the whale, began to pray for the Lord to set him free. And God, once again being the forgiving God that we know him to be, ordered the whale to "spit Jonah up on the beach." Again, the Lord told Jonah to go to Nineveh to carry the Lord's message. So Jonah obeyed the Lord, went to Nineveh, and preached to the people, "Nineveh will be destroyed in forty days."

The people of Nineveh believed the message of the Lord and immediately began to repent and fast and put on sackcloth to show that they had repented. Jonah became angry at the action of the people. He was so angry and unhappy that he proclaimed to the Lord, "Lord, let me die. I am better off dead than alive." In the end, Jonah showed more concern for a plant that died than for the entire people (120,000 in number) of Nineveh who had received God's message and repented. The lesson in the book is that God would rather forgive and save the enemies than to punish and destroy them.

DECEMBER 10
SCRIPTURE: JOHN 15:1 AND 5 (NRSV)

"I am the true vine, and my Father is the vine grower. He removes every branch in me that bears no fruit. I am the vine, you are the branches."

It's interesting to note when reading the gospels how Jesus used common items to illustrate His teaching. In the above scripture, He uses vines and branches. The vine is very productive, and proper cutting and pruning produces a good supply of grapes. The fruit of the vine, in that day, was symbolic of God's goodness to His people. God wants the branches (believers) to have a healthy attachment to the vine (Jesus) so that the plant is fruitful. Jesus is saying to the disciples (and us) that we must stay spiritually connected to Him. He also declares that apart from Him, "you can do nothing." God is glorified when we come into a righteous relationship with Him and bear much fruit in our lives.

DECEMBER 11
SCRIPTURE: MATTHEW 23:37 (NRSV)

"Jerusalem, Jerusalem, the city that kills the prophets and stones those who are sent to it! How often have I desired to gather your children together as a hen gathers her brood under her wings, and you were not willing!"

In Jesus' disappointment He doesn't rain down violence and destruction on the people. No! In typical Jesus-like fashion, He laments over the city of Jerusalem. He wants to gather up the people and protect and nurture them. What better way could Jesus illustrate His concern and love for them than to use how the mother hen draws her chicks under her protective wings! We today have that same offer to come under Jesus' love, warmth, and protection as did the believers of Jerusalem. That city was the capital city of God's chosen people. It was the ancestral home of David, Israel's greatest king, and the location of the Holy Temple, the earthly dwelling place of God. But the people of the city had become blind to God and insensitive to human needs. Many times we hurt but don't know to whom we should turn for help. But who knows us better than our creator? Those who turn to the Lord will find that He helps, comforts, and protects. Move under His wings!

DECEMBER 12
SCRIPTURE: JOHN 1:39 (TEV)

"'Come and see,' Jesus answered."

By the grace of God and the love of Jesus, this invitation remains open for each of us to come and see. He loves us so much that He dares not force us to Him. He gives us the free will to move to Him. He loves us to him! In fact, He loves us all the while.

I can remember specific times when Jesus extended the "come and see" invitation to me…not verbally, but through the love and actions of others. At age thirty-seven, I went to a lay-witness service at the Methodist church I attended in Decatur, Georgia, and heard a retired Marine colonel give his powerful testimony. Right in the middle of his witness, without benefit of music, he just broke into this song: "I have decided to follow Jesus, no turning back, no turning back."

Jesus spoke to me through that colonel's witness and I went to the altar. There I prayed, cried, and surrendered my life more completely and decided to follow Jesus in a more dedicated and committed fashion. My journey was again enriched by Jesus' invitation; and while I have ventured off the path many times, and will many more times, I can still hear those words, "no turning back, no turning back!"

Jesus had said, "Charles, come and see."

DECEMBER 13
SCRIPTURE: EPHESIANS 1:8-9 (NRSV)

"For it is by God's grace that you have been saved through faith. It is not the result of your own efforts, but God's gift, so that no one can boast about it."

No one can earn God's planned desire for us. He gives us eternal life when we experience Jesus and when we surrender to Him. This experience is the most important experience in our lives. It is such a revolutionary fact. We can't buy it or earn it! Romans 5:8 tells us, "God has shown us how much He loves us; it was while we were still sinners that Christ died for us." Scripture from Romans 10 tells us, "For it is by our faith that we are put right with God, it is by our confession that we are saved."

Perhaps this prayer to God would begin your surrender to Him. "Lord, come into my heart, take control of my life, and make me the person that you created me to be." You cannot earn your gift of a surrendered life.

DECEMBER 14
SCRIPTURE: 11 PETER 1:3 (NRSV)

"God's divine power has given us everything we need to live a truly religious life through our knowledge of the one who called us to share in His own glory and goodness."

Peter wants us to have a full measure of "everything we need to live a truly religious life." When we experience Jesus, we are given the knowledge and are empowered by the Holy Spirit to strengthen us to share His glory and divine nature. Peter suggests a list of Christ-like characteristics that are ours when we have experienced Jesus. Notice that these characteristics are listed in progressive fashion. This list begins with faith. Added are goodness, knowledge, self-control, endurance, Godliness, brotherly affection, and love. This progression involves growth on our part. We grow by exercising these qualities in our daily lives.

DECEMBER 15
SCRIPTURE: LUKE 1:34–35 (TEV)

"Mary said to the angel, 'I am a virgin. How, then, can this be? The angel answered, 'The Holy Spirit will come on you, and God's power will rest upon you. For this reason, the Holy Child will be called the Son of God.'"

We know from Luke's version of Jesus' birth the following facts about Mary, mother of Jesus. Mary was chosen by God to give birth to His son; Mary was told by an angel of God; Mary was a virgin; Mary obeyed God's plan; Mary praised God, saying, "My soul magnifies the Lord, and my spirit rejoices in God my Savior." And thus, Mary gave birth to her firstborn son and wrapped Him in bands of cloth, and laid Him in a manger, because there was no place for them in the Inn." And with the birth of Jesus, God changed the unveiling of history to offer us salvation and everlasting life. Praise God!

DECEMBER 16
SCRIPTURE: ROMANS 3:21–22 (NRSV)

"But now, apart from law, the righteousness of God has been disclosed, and is attested by the law and the prophets, the righteousness of God through faith in Jesus Christ for all who believe."

In our time something new has been added. What Moses and the prophets witnessed to all those years ago has happened. We now know that Jesus was about setting things right for us with God! He did it for us. Out of sheer generosity God puts us in the right standing with Himself, a pure gift! He got us out of the mess we were in and restored us to where He always wanted us to be. And He did it by means of Jesus Christ.

DECEMBER 17
SCRIPTURE: ROMANS 12:1 (TEV)

"So then, my brothers, because of God's great mercy to us I appeal to you: offer yourselves as a living sacrifice to God, dedicated to His service and pleasing to Him. This is the true worship that you should offer."

When we "offer ourselves" to God, we thereby surrender our life to the Lord. "Surrender" is not a popular word in our day and time. One definition is "to abandon or relinquish." We are taught from early childhood that to surrender is not the choice of actions that we should take. If you have ever watched small children in play groups, they do not want to share their toys with other children. So to surrender may be against our human nature…even as adults. We surrender ourselves to God, not because of fear or duty, but because of love. The Bible tells us "because He first loved us." The act of personal surrender to God is referred to as: consecration, making Jesus our Lord, taking up the cross, dying to self, yielding to the spirit. What really matters is that you do it. Pride may be a realistic barrier to your surrender. We want complete control. After all, haven't we been told often that we can pull ourselves up by our own bootstraps? We want to have it all and do it all! Victory comes through spiritual surrender. Surrender to the Lord and His way does not weaken you; it strengthens you! You will receive an everlasting crown!

DECEMBER 18
SCRIPTURE: LUKE 2:1–20 (READ) (NRSV)

You have just read "The Greatest Story Ever Told." Because of the gift Jesus Christ, God has changed the course of human affairs. In our individual lives, you and I can be reconciled back to the Father Himself. We can live Christ-like lives as God created us to be. There are so many examples of God's power and love reflected in just the above scripture. Advent hardly gives us time to ponder the full significance of God's plan for us! The words and actions of the above scripture are so impressed on our hearts that we can remember them always. We just need to worship God and give Him thanks in our daily prayers.

DECEMBER 19
SCRIPTURE: JOHN 1:4–5 (GOOD NEWS BIBLE)

"The word was the source of life and this life brought light to mankind. The light shines in the darkness, and the darkness has never put it out."

The Christmas story as told in the Gospels of Matthew and Luke demonstrates to me God's plan for reconciliation to Him in a story that we can all celebrate from ages two to ninety-two. It demonstrates God's mystery of angels, Mary, Joseph, the babe, the shepherds, the wise men, Herod, and a host of angelic beings singing, "Glory to God in the highest." We will always remember and enjoy the Christmas story for as long as we live!

But as Jesus began His ministry, the "John story" becomes especially meaningful. John tells us that Jesus became the light that this fallen world needed. Jesus is the real light—the light that comes into the world and shines on all mankind!

DECEMBER 20
SCRIPTURE: ISAIAH 9:6 (NRSV)

"For a child has been born for us, a son given to us; authority rests upon His shoulders; and He is named Wonderful Counselor, Mighty God, Everlasting Father, Prince of Peace."

The celebration of advent is recognized in Christian worship as the time for preparation of the coming of the Lord. The word "advent" means "to come." In "special ways" Christians come together each of the four Sundays, prior to Christmas Day, to prepare for the coming of Jesus Christ. The traditional manner of celebration is by use of a wreath in which five candles are placed. Four purple candles represent hope, love, joy, and peace. These four candles surround the fifth candle, which is white and represents Jesus Christ. On each of the four Sundays prior to Christmas, a candle is lighted. Then on Christmas Day the white candle in the middle of the wreath is lighted to represent Jesus, the light of the world. While the celebration of advent is a New Testament worship tradition, it has its roots of prophecy in the Old Testament. Jesus Himself in the last chapter of Revelation, verse 16: "I am the root and descendant of David, the bright and morning star." Praise God!

DECEMBER 21
SCRIPTURE: LUKE 2:38 (NRSV)

"Then Mary said to the Angel Gabriel, here I am, the servant of the Lord; let it be with me according to your word. Then the Angel departed from her."

The angel Gabriel had announced to Mary that the virgin birth would become a reality to her. And in verses 46-48 (same chapter): "Mary gave her song of praise to the Lord." And Mary said, "My soul magnifies the Lord, and my spirit rejoices in God my Savior. For He has looked with favor on the lowliness of His servant. Surely, from now and all generations will call me blessed; for the mighty one has done great things for me, and Holy is His name!" Let us behold the Lamb of God!

DECEMBER 22
SCRIPTURE: JOHN 3:16 (NRSV)

"For God so loved the world."

Isn't it amazing that God had His son placed in a stable at birth? His son joined a family who was not considered as royalty. He lived and grew up as a carpenter, and yet brought to the world a new and radical form of love that has lasted for over two thousand years. God became a member of family, our family, and we became a member of God's community, a community of believers. Celebrate your family. Tell them how much God loves them and how much you love them. Let your family know that they are God's gift to you.

DECEMBER 23
SCRIPTURE: PSALM 98:1 (GOOD NEWS BIBLE)

"Sing a new song to the Lord; He has done wonderful things!"

Christmas choirs and congregations sing a new song to God as they gather each December to celebrate the birth of Jesus. On Christmas Day we hear the story of God entering the world in the flesh—the very world He had created.

Through songs and Psalms humankind gives witness to the music and majesty with which the earth responds to God.

The Christmas favorite, "Joy to the World," was written from an inspiration of reading Psalm 98. Isaac Watt wrote this much loved hymn in 1719.

Through the works of poets and musicians we hear the message of Christmas Day proclaimed in a new way: "Joy to the world—Joy to the world, the Lord has come. Let earth receive her King!"

DECEMBER 24
SCRIPTURE: LUKE 2:6–7 (NRSV)

"And Mary gave birth to her firstborn son and wrapped in bands of cloth, and laid Him in a manger, because there was no place for them in the inn."

Because of God's gift of Jesus Christ, the whole course of human affairs was changed. Humankind (you and me) can now be reconciled with God. We can now live Christ-like lives centered around hope, love, joy, and peace. Jesus Christ has "exercised His might in the world as a power and influence unequaled by the combined influence and power of all the famous monarchs, statesmen, generals, inventors, authors and (presidents) that the world has even seen." Joy to the world!

DECEMBER 25
SCRIPTURE: MATTHEW 1:19 AND 20 (TEV)

"This was how the birth of Jesus Christ took place. His mother, Mary, was engaged to Joseph, but before they were married, she found out that she was going to have a baby by the Holy Spirit. An angel of the Lord appeared in a dream and said to Joseph, 'Do not be afraid to take Mary to be your wife. For it is by the Holy Spirit that she has conceived.'"

Little is known about Joseph, and many may consider him as the forgotten man at Christmas. However, there is much to learn from the great faith of Joseph. In him can be seen qualities that challenge us to deeper faith, obedience, and love.

In scripture, we learn these three qualities about Joseph. He learned to listen to others and to God. He learned to obey God in making his decisions. He knew to honor God's will in living out his life. Surely, Jesus learned much about His heavenly Father from His earthly Father, Joseph. Like Joseph, we can learn to exemplify the God-like qualities that lead us to deeper levels of faith, obedience, and love.

DECEMBER 26
SCRIPTURE: LUKE 2:21 (TEV)

"A week later, when the time came for the baby to be circumcised, He was named Jesus, the name which the angel had given Him before He had been conceived."

"Immanuel, God with us." "Jesus, the one who saves." These are the names of the Incarnate God, given by a community of angels.

When Jesus was given His name, humankind's relationship with God changed. The God of mystery and divine distance became a God who walked among the people. From this point on, we have been on a first-name basis with God. We celebrate the new name given to God of the universe—the Holy name of Jesus.

The child of Mary and Joseph was given a Holy name that carries the promise of salvation. They called Him "Immanuel, God with us." They praised Him as a Wonderful Counselor, Mighty God, Everlasting Father.

This child was to be called Jesus—"He who saves."

DECEMBER 27
SCRIPTURE: MATTHEW 19:14 (NIV)

"Jesus said, 'Let the little children come to me, and do not hinder them, for the kingdom of heaven belongs to such as these.'"

At a luncheon meeting, there was a young mother who brought her five-year-old daughter. The fellowship hall was a hive of noise and work as the guests lined up to serve themselves lunch from the buffet. The child became restless and irritable, and finally, the mother placed her in "time out" right next to the old piano in the room. She continued to cry softly to herself until the pastor, feeling sorry for the child, asked the mother if he could take her into the sanctuary to show her something. With her approval, he asked the little girl to come with him. Holding her hand, he led her to the nativity scene, placed in a corner of the sanctuary. She stared at it in awe as the pastor told her who the figures were. And at last, he came to the baby Jesus and she whispered, "Can I touch Him?" "Sure," replied the pastor. Her eyes lit up and she smiled. "Oh, Baby Jesus!" She went back to the luncheon and told her mother, "Momma, I touched the Baby Jesus." She was a quiet and pleasant child for the rest of the luncheon and meeting.

The Baby Jesus can do that to one's heart—give you peace, serenity, and joy! Hallelujah!

DECEMBER 28
SCRIPTURE: MATTHEW 1:23 (TEV)

"Jesus will be called Immanuel which means, God is with us."

Do we really comprehend the full significance of the events of the Christmas story? It is an amazing story replayed for each of us, each year of our lives...and it will be repeated every year as long as we live. The disciple, John, introduces us to Jesus in the first chapter, verses 4 and 5. He states, "Jesus is the word and the source of life, and this life brought light to humankind. The light shines in the darkness, and the darkness has never put it out." Jesus provides us with... light for the way; grace for the trials; help from above; unfailing sympathy; and undying love.

DECEMBER 29
SCRIPTURE: ROMANS 12:15–16 (TEV)

"Be happy with those who are happy. Weep with those who weep. Have the same concern for everyone."

I hope that each is able to look to this coming year with great expectations. That we are able to look beyond the pain of our own bodies, beyond the hurt of another's words, beyond the selfishness of too much gain, beyond the loss of family and friends, beyond the loss of control brought about by aging, and that we will be able to steadfastly focus our lives on the joy of living. Think of joy as an acronym formed from the first letters of Jesus, Others, and You. Joy! Each of us is only one individual; how do we concentrate on events of a world nature?

We don't have to plan our year on grand, worldly acts; only on Jesus, others, and you. By doing that, we reduce our task drastically. I hope you find joy in your life.

DECEMBER 30
SCRIPTURE: NUMBERS 6:24–26 (TEV)

"May the Lord bless you and take care of you; may the Lord be kind and gracious to you; may the Lord look on you with favor and give you peace."

The word "peace" is found over 400 times in the Bible. It is a major concern to the Holy Trinity! Spiritual peace is a state of being that gives one rest and that promotes harmony, tranquility, and serenity. It is not necessarily an automatic state—peace requires much action and prayers on our part. Many conditions in our lives cause us to deviate from harmony and serenity. Even though we know that God wants us to be at peace, and even though we know that being in a peaceful state reduces our own fears, anxieties, troubles, and doubts. We still find that these do not render peace to our hearts, minds, or souls. Jesus wants us to be at peace, but He wants us to have a faith-filled desire to attain that which He tells us in scripture is ours. He states, "Peace is what I leave you." Jesus wants what is best for us. May it be so for you and for me.

DECEMBER 31
SCRIPTURE: LUKE 1:26 (NRSV)

"Let it be with me according to your word."

We live in troubled times—Christians under attack, the decline of marriage, political upheavals and worse, so much that threatens our way of life!

During this last week of the year, we wonder what the new year holds for us. Do we have answers? Do we have hope? Look back at Mary's statement to the angel: "let it be with me according to your word!" Her statement certainly holds promise for us two thousand years later! Mary simply relied on her faith in God. If you believe in the Bible, as the authentic word of God, then you will have answers to your questions and solutions to your problems. Did you know there are 901 promises that God gives us in the Bible?

For the upcoming year, I would strongly urge you to break out your Bible, and refer to God's words to enhance and encourage you in your daily life. Don't just leave it on the coffee table—use it as your guide for the journey of a new year and a new way of living.

AUTHOR'S NOTE

It has been said that God fleshes out His love best to His precious humankind through family. That certainly has been true of my family. Throughout the months of my cancer treatment and recovery, my wife Carolyn, and our three children and their spouses, Christopher and Carolyn, Corey and Stephanie, and Cameron and Will, have held me closely in their prayers and in their tender, loving care. Additionally, my three brothers and their spouses and four of my favorite cousins have been right there beside me with love and care.

In the experience of writing this book, my wife, Carolyn, read and re-read the 365 devotions at least three times each. Also, I must point out the invaluable assistance of my son, Christopher, who took on this adventure with determination and expertise. He guided the whole process.

My appreciation and deep love to each of these family members.

ACKNOWLEDGEMENTS

The author is grateful for the generosity of many people who touched this project.

The remarkable painting on the cover of this book was created by Jack Garner. It is part of the Stations of the Cross collection at St. Peter's Episcopal Church in Oxford, Mississippi. The Rector of St. Peter's, the Rev. Jody Burnett, was very supportive in allowing us to use the painting. The team at the University of Mississippi's Marketing and Communications Department photographed the painting.

The book was designed by the talented Rebecca Hollis, of New Orleans, with additional production assistance by Ted Hill and the team at The Ramey Agency in Jackson.

Corey Ray took the author photograph on the back cover.

This book would not have been published without the help of Neil White, author of the memoir, *In the Sanctuary of Outcasts*, and publisher at Nautilus Publishing Company in Oxford, Mississippi. Neil provided advice and counsel throughout the journey, helping us navigate our way in unchartered waters.

Made in the USA
Lexington, KY
21 December 2019